MAJOR WORLD LEADERS

KING ABDULLAH II
YASIR ARAFAT
BASHAR al-ASSAD
MENACHEM BEGIN
SILVIO BERLUSCONI
TONY BLAIR
GEORGE W. BUSH
JIMMY CARTER
FIDEL CASTRO
RECEP TAYYIP ERDOĞAN
VICENTE FOX
SADDAM HUSSEIN
HAMID KARZAI
KIM IL SUNG AND KIM JONG IL
HOSNI MUBARAK
PERVEZ MUSHARRAF
VLADIMIR PUTIN
MOHAMMED REZA PAHLAVI
ANWAR SADAT
THE SAUDI ROYAL FAMILY
GERHARD SCHROEDER
ARIEL SHARON
LUIZ INÁCIO LULA DA SILVA
MUAMMAR QADDAFI

MAJOR WORLD LEADERS

Muammar Qaddafi

Brenda Lange

Philadelphia

Cover: Muammar Qaddafi, in uniform, 1981.

Frontispiece: Muammar Qaddafi, in uniform, 1985.

CHELSEA HOUSE PUBLISHERS

V.P., NEW PRODUCT DEVELOPMENT Sally Cheney
DIRECTOR OF PRODUCTION Kim Shinners
CREATIVE MANAGER Takeshi Takahashi
MANUFACTURING MANAGER Diann Grasse

Staff for MUAMMAR QADDAFI

EXECUTIVE EDITOR Lee Marcott
EDITORIAL ASSISTANT Carla Greenberg
PRODUCTION EDITOR Noelle Nardone
PICTURE RESEARCH Robin Bonner
INTERIOR DESIGN Takeshi Takahashi
COVER DESIGN Keith Trego
LAYOUT 21st Century Publishing and Communications, Inc.

©2005 by Chelsea House Publishers, a subsidiary of Haights Cross Communications. All rights reserved. Printed and bound in China.

A Haights Cross Communications Company

http://www.chelseahouse.com

First Printing

1 3 5 7 9 8 6 4 2

Library of Congress Cataloging-in-Publication Data

Lange, Brenda.
   Muammar Qaddafi / Brenda Lange.
      p. cm.—(Major world leaders)
Includes bibliographical references and index.
   ISBN 0-7910-8258-X (hardcover)
 1. Libya—Juvenile literature. 2. Qaddafi, Muammar—Juvenile literature. I. Title. II. Series.
DT215.L35 2005
961.204'2'092—dc22
                                                                    2004024077

All links and web addresses were checked and verified to be correct at the time of publication. Because of the dynamic nature of the web, some addresses and links may have changed since publication and may no longer be valid.

TABLE OF CONTENTS

	Foreword: On Leadership Arthur M. Schlesinger, jr.	6
1	Can a Tiger Really Change His Stripes?	12
2	Libya's History, Culture, Religion, People	20
3	Who is Muammar Qaddafi?	32
4	Government—Qaddafi's Way	41
5	Oil and Water: A Potent Economic Combination for Libya	52
6	Never-ending Battles with the Rest of the World	61
7	Qaddafi's Sponsorship of Terrorism	70
8	Fallout from Terrorist Activities: Sanctions and Military Actions	80
9	Libya Today and Qaddafi's Legacy	93
	Chronology	106
	Further Reading	107
	Index	108

On Leadership

Arthur M. Schlesinger, jr.

Leadership, it may be said, is really what makes the world go round. Love no doubt smoothes the passage; but love is a private transaction between consenting adults. Leadership is a public transaction with history. The idea of leadership affirms the capacity of individuals to move, inspire, and mobilize masses of people so that they act together in pursuit of an end. Sometimes leadership serves good purposes, sometimes bad; but whether the end is benign or evil, great leaders are those men and women who leave their personal stamp on history.

Now, the very concept of leadership implies the proposition that individuals can make a difference. This proposition has never been universally accepted. From classical times to the present day, eminent thinkers have regarded individuals as no more than the agents and pawns of larger forces, whether the gods and goddesses of the ancient world or, in the modern era, race, class, nation, the dialectic, the will of the people, the spirit of the times, history itself. Against such forces, the individual dwindles into insignificance.

So contends the thesis of historical determinism. Tolstoy's great novel *War and Peace* offers a famous statement of the case. Why, Tolstoy asked, did millions of men in the Napoleonic Wars, denying their human feelings and their common sense, move back and forth across Europe slaughtering their fellows? "The war," Tolstoy answered, "was bound to happen simply because it was bound to happen." All prior history determined it. As for leaders, they, Tolstoy said, "are but the labels that serve to give a name to an end and, like labels, they have the least possible connection with the event." The greater the leader, "the more conspicuous the inevitability and the predestination of every act he commits." The leader, said Tolstoy, is "the slave of history."

Determinism takes many forms. Marxism is the determinism of class. Nazism the determinism of race. But the idea of men and women as the slaves of history runs athwart the deepest human instincts. Rigid determinism abolishes the idea of human freedom—the assumption of free choice that underlies every move we make, every word we speak, every thought we think. It abolishes the idea of human responsibility, since it is manifestly unfair to reward or punish people for actions that are by definition beyond their control. No one can live consistently by any deterministic creed. The Marxist states prove this themselves by their extreme susceptibility to the cult of leadership.

More than that, history refutes the idea that individuals make no difference. In December 1931 a British politician crossing Fifth Avenue in New York City between 76th and 77th Streets around 10:30 P.M. looked in the wrong direction and was knocked down by an automobile— a moment, he later recalled, of a man aghast, a world aglare: "I do not understand why I was not broken like an eggshell or squashed like a gooseberry." Fourteen months later an American politician, sitting in an open car in Miami, Florida, was fired on by an assassin; the man beside him was hit. Those who believe that individuals make no difference to history might well ponder whether the next two decades would have been the same had Mario Constasino's car killed Winston Churchill in 1931 and Giuseppe Zangara's bullet killed Franklin Roosevelt in 1933. Suppose, in addition, that Lenin had died of typhus in Siberia in 1895 and that Hitler had been killed on the Western Front in 1916. What would the 20th century have looked like now?

For better or for worse, individuals do make a difference. "The notion that a people can run itself and its affairs anonymously," wrote the philosopher William James, "is now well known to be the silliest of absurdities. Mankind does nothing save through initiatives on the part of inventors, great or small, and imitation by the rest of us—these are the sole factors in human progress. Individuals of genius show the way, and set the patterns, which common people then adopt and follow."

Leadership, James suggests, means leadership in thought as well as in action. In the long run, leaders in thought may well make the greater difference to the world. "The ideas of economists and political philosophers, both when they are right and when they are wrong," wrote John Maynard Keynes, "are more powerful than is commonly understood. Indeed the world is ruled by little else. Practical men, who believe themselves to be quite exempt from any intellectual influences, are usually the slaves of some defunct economist. . . . The power of vested interests is vastly exaggerated compared with the gradual encroachment of ideas."

But, as Woodrow Wilson once said, "Those only are leaders of men, in the general eye, who lead in action.... It is at their hands that new thought gets its translation into the crude language of deeds." Leaders in thought often invent in solitude and obscurity, leaving to later generations the tasks of imitation. Leaders in action—the leaders portrayed in this series—have to be effective in their own time.

And they cannot be effective by themselves. They must act in response to the rhythms of their age. Their genius must be adapted, in a phrase from William James, "to the receptivities of the moment." Leaders are useless without followers. "There goes the mob," said the French politician, hearing a clamor in the streets. "I am their leader. I must follow them." Great leaders turn the inchoate emotions of the mob to purposes of their own. They seize on the opportunities of their time, the hopes, fears, frustrations, crises, potentialities. They succeed when events have prepared the way for them, when the community is awaiting to be aroused, when they can provide the clarifying and organizing ideas. Leadership completes the circuit between the individual and the mass and thereby alters history.

It may alter history for better or for worse. Leaders have been responsible for the most extravagant follies and most monstrous crimes that have beset suffering humanity. They have also been vital in such gains as humanity has made in individual freedom, religious and racial tolerance, social justice, and respect for human rights.

There is no sure way to tell in advance who is going to lead for good and who for evil. But a glance at the gallery of men and women in MAJOR WORLD LEADERS suggests some useful tests.

One test is this: Do leaders lead by force or by persuasion? By command or by consent? Through most of history leadership was exercised by the divine right of authority. The duty of followers was to defer and to obey. "Theirs not to reason why/Theirs but to do and die." On occasion, as with the so-called enlightened despots of the 18th century in Europe, absolutist leadership was animated by humane purposes. More often, absolutism nourished the passion for domination, land, gold, and conquest and resulted in tyranny.

The great revolution of modern times has been the revolution of equality. "Perhaps no form of government," wrote the British historian James Bryce in his study of the United States, *The American Commonwealth*, "needs great leaders so much as democracy." The idea that all people should be equal in their legal condition has undermined the old structure of authority, hierarchy, and deference. The revolution of equality has had two contrary effects on the nature of leadership. For equality, as Alexis de Tocqueville pointed out in his great study *Democracy in America*, might mean equality in servitude as well as equality in freedom.

"I know of only two methods of establishing equality in the political world," Tocqueville wrote. "Rights must be given to every citizen, or none at all to anyone . . . save one, who is the master of all." There was no middle ground "between the sovereignty of all and the absolute power of one man." In his astonishing prediction of 20th-century totalitarian dictatorship, Tocqueville explained how the revolution of equality could lead to the *Führerprinzip* and more terrible absolutism than the world had ever known.

But when rights are given to every citizen and the sovereignty of all is established, the problem of leadership takes a new form, becomes more exacting than ever before. It is easy to issue commands and enforce them by the rope and the stake, the concentration camp and the *gulag*. It is much harder to use argument and achievement to overcome opposition and win consent. The Founding Fathers of the United States understood the difficulty. They believed that history had given them the opportunity to decide, as Alexander Hamilton wrote in the first Federalist Paper, whether men are indeed capable of basing government on "reflection and choice, or whether they are forever destined to depend . . . on accident and force."

Government by reflection and choice called for a new style of leadership and a new quality of followership. It required leaders to be responsive to popular concerns, and it required followers to be active and informed participants in the process. Democracy does not eliminate emotion from politics; sometimes it fosters demagoguery; but it is confident that, as the greatest of democratic leaders put it, you cannot fool all of the people all of the time. It measures leadership by results and retires those who overreach or falter or fail.

It is true that in the long run despots are measured by results too. But they can postpone the day of judgment, sometimes indefinitely, and in the meantime they can do infinite harm. It is also true that democracy is no guarantee of virtue and intelligence in government, for the voice of the people is not necessarily the voice of God. But democracy, by assuring the right of opposition, offers built-in resistance to the evils inherent in absolutism. As the theologian Reinhold Niebuhr summed it up, "Man's capacity for justice makes democracy possible, but man's inclination to justice makes democracy necessary."

A second test for leadership is the end for which power is sought. When leaders have as their goal the supremacy of a master race or the promotion of totalitarian revolution or the acquisition and exploitation of colonies or the protection of greed and privilege or the preservation of personal power, it is likely that their leadership will do little to advance the cause of humanity. When their goal is the abolition of slavery, the liberation of women, the enlargement of opportunity for the poor and powerless, the extension of equal rights to racial minorities, the defense of the freedoms of expression and opposition, it is likely that their leadership will increase the sum of human liberty and welfare.

Leaders have done great harm to the world. They have also conferred great benefits. You will find both sorts in this series. Even "good" leaders must be regarded with a certain wariness. Leaders are not demigods; they put on their trousers one leg after another just like ordinary mortals. No leader is infallible, and every leader needs to be reminded of this at regular intervals. Irreverence irritates leaders but is their salvation. Unquestioning submission corrupts leaders and demeans followers. Making a cult of a leader is always a mistake. Fortunately hero worship generates its own antidote. "Every hero," said Emerson, "becomes a bore at last."

The signal benefit the great leaders confer is to embolden the rest of us to live according to our own best selves, to be active, insistent, and resolute in affirming our own sense of things. For great leaders attest to the reality of human freedom against the supposed inevitabilities of history. And they attest to the wisdom and power that may lie within the most unlikely of us, which is why Abraham Lincoln remains the supreme example of great leadership. A great leader, said Emerson, exhibits new possibilities to all humanity. "We feed on genius. . . . Great men exist that there may be greater men."

Great leaders, in short, justify themselves by emancipating and empowering their followers. So humanity struggles to master its destiny, remembering with Alexis de Tocqueville: "It is true that around every man a fatal circle is traced beyond which he cannot pass; but within the wide verge of that circle he is powerful and free; as it is with man, so with communities."

CHAPTER

1

Can a Tiger Really Change His Stripes?

Colonel Muammar Qaddafi strode onto the stage in the spring of 2004, quieting the vast crowd merely with his presence. This enigmatic man, the leader of Libya since 1969, an outspoken supporter of worldwide terrorism, and an avid anti-Western Muslim, was about to stun the world with his words.

Elegantly attired in a navy blue uniform complete with epaulets, gold braid, and a sash around his waist, Qaddafi demanded attention with his appearance. The half-dozen or so female members of his personal guard, wearing their camouflage uniforms and signature red berets, surrounded him and scanned the crowd for any sign of danger.

As Qaddafi began to speak, the silence of the crowd was complete. This speech, however, was different from those he normally delivered. It was not full of hatred and anger toward the West, covering his

Can a Tiger Really Change His Stripes? 13

Libyan leader Muammar Qaddafi, February 2004. Qaddafi, commonly referred to in Libya as "The Leader," looks to the future in his hometown of Sirte, Libya. Colonel Qaddafi, who first came to power during a military coup on September 1, 1969, spent most of his rule preaching anti-American rhetoric. Since December 2003, however, he has sought to strengthen Libya's relationship with the United States.

usual few topics—anything anti-Israel, anti-Egyptian, and anti-American. This time Qaddafi's speech offered apologies, and accepted blame.

The leader the world has known as a "madman" seems to have changed his course, recently offering voluntary disarmament and moderating his extremist views. But is this offer valid? Is the about-face to be believed? Or is it a ruse for worse behavior to come?

As a young revolutionary, Qaddafi had a brilliant military mind and was a master of manipulation. He turned a group of schoolboy pals into a well-trained cadre of soldiers who overthrew the monarchy and took control of the country. The government he formed—the *Jamahiriya*, roughly translated to "the state of the masses"—looked promising for a time. Some of the problems caused by the reign of King Idris I and his cronies were rectified as money came pouring into the country from the discovery of oil.

Qaddafi did indeed share the newfound oil wealth. Better education, rebuilt roads, and modern housing were among the improvements that Libya's citizens saw after Qaddafi came to power. Women's rights improved, and Libya became an international economic force.

He wrote a three-volume guide called *The Green Book* in which he lay out government, Qaddafi-style. Based on the *Shariah*, or the laws of Islam, *The Green Book* outlined his philosophies of government and society. In it, Qaddafi presented his "Third Universal Theory," a blend of socialism, Arab nationalism, and populism that was intended to guide the people in self-rule. He referred to Libya as an "imaginary island . . . enjoying a perfect social, legal, and political system."

But his vehemence was total toward any country that he perceived as anti-Arab and/or pro-Israel, like the United States, Britain, France, and Italy. His nationalism and belief in a united Arab nation was nearly as all-consuming.

Several terrorist attacks in the mid-1980s, including bombings in airports in Vienna and Rome and in a West Berlin disco, were connected to terrorists whom Qaddafi sponsored. These violent acts resulted in economic sanctions against Libya by the United States and American air strikes against the country in 1986. Tripoli, the capital, and Benghazi, the second-largest

Can a Tiger Really Change His Stripes?

A young woman studies the philosophy of Libyan leader Muammar Qaddafi at the Green Book Center in Tripoli. A ceiling-high portrait of the leader looks on. *The Green Book*, translated by the Libyan government into 53 languages, is a 1970s tract on Qaddafi's philosophy.

city, were attacked, and Qaddafi's adopted 15-month-old daughter was killed.

The world recoiled after Libyan intelligence officers were implicated in two of the worst acts of terrorism the world had known before September 11, 2001. Those attacks, the bombing of Pan Am Flight 103 over Lockerbie, Scotland, which killed 270 people in December 1988, and the destruction of a French airplane the following year, which killed 171 people, ended tolerance toward the man President Ronald Reagan had called "the mad dog of the Middle East."

Sanctions imposed by the United Nations and the United States ultimately strangled the country and reduced it to a level of poverty unknown since before the discovery of oil in the late 1950s. Qaddafi's extreme methods eventually earned him the disdain of his fellow Arab leaders. Even Egypt backed away, and Qaddafi had based his revolution on the beliefs of that nation's former president. This distancing was one of the factors that led Qaddafi to approach the United States with open arms, and open access to his weapons programs.

Qaddafi may have felt his methods were the best means to an end: his goal of one Arab state. Other Arab leaders may have agreed with him in theory, but none wanted to give up their power. During the U.S. bombing of Tripoli in 1986, these countries were quick to offer verbal support and encouragement but were not forthcoming in ways that would have counted—with troops and weapons. The Soviet Union, too—until then one of Libya's biggest supporters, providing equipment, troops, and valuable advisers—kept its distance, arriving in Tripoli well after the fighting had ended.

Even the groups that Qaddafi had supported for years, including the Palestine Liberation Organization, the Irish Republican Army and the African National Congress, all had begun to negotiate with their old enemies, leaving Qaddafi isolated in his extremism, with no one left to support. Libya's economy and people suffered for his stubbornness.

A "NEW ERA"

The broad sanctions imposed by the United Nations remained in place until September 2003 when Libya acknowledged responsibility for the Pan Am attack and agreed to pay compensation to its victims' families. Most of the U.S. sanctions, however, remained in place until April 2004 as leverage to force Libya to admit to its proliferation of weapons of mass destruction and give up its programs involving chemical, biological, and nuclear weapons.

In March 2003, right after the United States invaded Iraq, Libya entered into talks with Britain, offering to rid itself of "unconventional weapons if it would lead to diplomatic relations, trade, and investment with the United States." On December 19, 2003, Libya announced to the world that it was giving up all development of weapons of mass destruction. Rather than end up like Saddam Hussein, hiding in a hole in the desert, Qaddafi decided he would rather pass along his power to his son.

Then, early in 2004, Qaddafi made his historic speech outlining a "new era." To an audience composed of his General People's Congress, the world press, and an American contingent of politicians, he declared that "the world has changed" and his country needed to adapt to "the new realities." According to *U.S. News & World Report*, "he admitted that it is Libya that isolated itself for the sake of others, and he asked whether Libya should persist in being more Palestinian than the Palestinians or more Irish than the Irish. He said Libya's quest for chemical and nuclear weapons had brought danger, not security."

In a few short months, according to a June 2004 article in *U.S. News & World Report*, the Libyan government wasted no time in living up to its disarmament pledge: "Atomic bomb designs, tons of centrifuge parts, tanks of uranium hexafluoride gas, and other nuclear gear are under lock and key in U.S. government warehouses in Tennessee.... Thirty-three hundred munitions designed to hold chemical agents have been crushed and 26 tons of mustard gas secured for future disposal. A chemical factory at Rabta, south of Tripoli, will be converted solely to pharmaceutical production."

The Libyans also have disclosed information on nuclear supply networks and weapons facilities. The U.S. government is moving carefully in removing sanctions and reinstating diplomatic ties. According to *U.S. News & World Report*, the goal is to "leverage Libya's thirst for American technology and investment into further concessions."

Washington's acceptance of Qaddafi's apparent change of governing style and voluntary disarmament comes at a cost. It means that Qaddafi will continue to rule the country he has for so long, perhaps passing the reins to one of his sons. But according to U.S. officials, it is important that a message be sent to other countries with anti-American leanings: A reward is waiting for those who move to cooperate with the West and act in a more globally responsible fashion.

International officials and media pundits have called Qaddafi's changes a "growing-up process." Perhaps he has realized that his country, which he took on a roller-coaster ride from poor and poorly run to rich and prosperous and back to poverty again, could not exist much longer in its current state.

In early 2004, Libya's unemployment rate was about 25 percent (higher for young workers), its infrastructure and neighborhoods were crumbling, and worst of all, oil production was cut in half. These conditions would combine to drive the people to revolt in the streets. Perhaps Qaddafi looked toward his legacy and simply could not bear to have future generations view him negatively. But even with Qaddafi's apparent newfound openness, his government, for all intents and purposes, remains a dictatorship.

Is it really possible for Qaddafi to give up the amount of control required for Libya truly to become a democratic society? Despite calling his government a Jamahiriya, and despite the existence of local people's committees, which masquerade as direct democracy, is true democratic rule possible with Qaddafi still in power?

Learning more about the forces that shaped Muammar Qaddafi in his childhood and young adulthood and about the country of his birth and its history may help answer some of these questions.

CHAPTER

2

Libya's History, Culture, Religion, People

Libya is built on ancient land, with a rich history and culture to match. Ancient Libya was populated by Stone Age man, proven by the stone knives and hammers, pottery, cooking utensils, and spearheads excavated by archaeologists. Rock paintings date back 4,000 to 5,000 years. The people were hunter-gatherers who had not yet learned to raise animals or to farm. These people, known as Berbers, established Libya's first recorded civilization. They originally settled along the coastline and eventually moved inland where they learned to farm and herd animals. Three main groups formed later: the Luata, the Nefusa, and the Adassa, whose distinctive tribal customs still can be identified.

The Phoenicians, who came from Tyre in what is now Lebanon, were traders, sailors, and warriors. They were an advanced people who founded Carthage and eventually ruled many North African

Libya's History, Culture, Religion, People

The Roman amphitheatre of the ancient city of Sabratha, 42 miles (67 kilometers) west of the Libyan capital, Tripoli, on the Mediterranean coast. The city was one of the major gateways to the caravan routes to African and other areas. Rome, only one of many foreign countries to occupy Libya, invaded the country in 46 B.C. and ruled there for 500 years.

countries. Libya became their central trading post from which they traveled to other lands and traded jewelry, clothes, and weapons for ivory, gold dust, and ostrich feathers. They also established a slave route that lasted for 2,000 years. The Phoenicians traveled the sea as pirates, attacking merchant ships and forcing the Berbers to serve them as sailors. In 46 B.C., the Phoenicians were conquered by the Romans, who went on to rule Libya for the next 500 years. Libya flourished under Roman rule.

Libya's history continued to be dominated by the tribe or country that was strong enough to evict the previous conqueror. The Vandals took over Libya in 435 A.D. and, as accomplished cartographers, mapped the country and its waterways. A mere 100 years later, the Vandals were overthrown by the Turks, who were in turn overthrown about 90 years after that by Egyptian Arabs. Until this point, the Libyan people had managed to acclimate themselves to whoever came along, but the Egyptian Arabs were cruel, destroying everything in their path.

The Berbers fought back by forming small groups, hiding in the mountains and deserts, and then staging guerrilla attacks on the Arabs. The Arabs were not to be defeated, however, and ruled Libya until 800. Tunisian troops expelled the Arabs and ruled until 909. Over the next two centuries, other Arab groups controlled Libya, but it was the Arab conquerors in the eleventh century who came peacefully and gradually assimilated with Berber society. The Berbers adopted Islam, the religion of the Arabs, and their language. Today nearly 97 percent of Libyans are Arabic-speaking Muslims of mixed Arab and Berber descent. The word "Arab" generally refers to anyone from the Middle East or North Africa for whom Arabic is their native tongue. By this definition, there are nearly 300 million Arabs worldwide.

Libyans are naturally suspicious of outsiders and are resistant to change. These traits probably arose because their country has been overrun so often and ruled by foreigners for so long. Even so, Libyans have managed to maintain a fierce level of tribal pride and independence. Long before the advent of Muammar Qaddafi, the people of this region were traditionalists who prized their long-held tribal rituals and beliefs. The tribe, or *qabilah*, takes precedence over the individual. It is a "unit that prizes its own laws, rules, religious practices, rites, traditions and pecking order above any that might be imposed from the outside," according to Ted Gottfried in his book,

Libya: Desert Land in Conflict. He added, "The tribe cares for its children and commands their respect. It honors its old people and values their experience and wisdom." It was this sense of continuity and pride in tradition that Qaddafi espoused in his push toward nationalism and a pan-Arab state.

INDEPENDENCE

During World War II, fierce fighting took place in Northern Africa between the Allied forces—Britain, France, and the United States—and the European Axis of Germany and Italy. The Libyans saw the chance to take back their country from Italy and organized an army to support the Allies. By 1943, the Allies had liberated the country, and Great Britain and France administered the country for a time.

Shortly after the end of the war, Italy renounced its claims to the territory. The United States, Great Britain, France, and Russia signed a treaty in 1947 agreeing to determine Libya's future. These allies found it difficult to chart Libya's course since it had strategic importance, with its untapped natural resources and its location on the Mediterranean shipping lanes. In 1949, the United Nations called for the establishment of an independent state in Libya. Two years later, a national assembly was established, and a constitution of independence was written and adopted. The country was named the United Kingdom of Libya, and set up as a monarchy under the rule of King Idris I. This was the first time the country had been united, rather than existing as three colonies—Tripolitania, Cyrenaica, and Fezzan—and ruled by another country.

King Idris's authority was challenged in two of the regions—Tripolitania and Fezzan—but he held firm and declared that Allah had given him absolute religious authority. When Idris declared that city life was "degenerate," he also alienated the residents of Tripoli and Benghazi.

The king, however, was a hypocrite. While he withheld luxurious living from his people, maintaining that fine clothing

Libya's King Idris I, during the opening of Libya's first parliament in Benghazi, March 25, 1952. When oil was discovered on Libyan land in 1959, the resulting wealth was hoarded by Idris and his associates, despite the poverty of the masses, and this eventually led to his downfall.

and food were sinful, he indulged in every little luxury available, including fine palaces, fancy foods and clothing, and recreation. To maintain his lavish lifestyle, he rented space for military bases to the British and Americans.

Once oil was discovered, Idris found he had enough revenue to indulge his every whim and those of his family and friends. By 1964 he had expelled the British from the country. Even though the American military was allowed to remain for a time, the U.S. government began to view Idris as a "loose cannon" who might, at any time, decide to align with the Soviet Union, selling it the precious oil that the United States and Britain wanted. It was well known that Idris was keeping most of the oil income. The people remained poor, and they blamed

Idris as he tightened his rule by repealing the federal constitution and naming himself the sole ruler. A Socialist movement began, growing wider and creating fertile ground from which Qaddafi's group would spring.

RELIGION

About 97 percent of Libyans are Muslims, but before Islam was introduced in the seventh century, the Berbers practiced different religions. Some were animists, or those who worship nature, who believe that everything has a soul—from rocks, trees, and the stars to all plants and animals. They believe that all these souls are interconnected, and some believe that these interconnected souls form one universal soul. Other tribes practiced ancestor worship, in which their dead ancestors had godlike powers. Others prayed to the spirits of the rain and other aspects of nature.

About 3 percent of Libyans are Roman Catholics or Jews. The balance of the population is Sunni Muslim, the largest group within the Muslim religion. Even though they are traditionalists, they are considered to be mainstream. Sunni Muslims strongly resent Israel because they feel it is a country stolen from Muslims with the backing of European and American Christians. The Libyan *imams*, or Islamic holy leaders, assure their people that the battle to return Israeli lands to the Palestinians is noble and blessed by God; what they call a holy war or *jihad*.

The other Muslim branch is the Shiite sect, which has a different conception of who Muhammad's spiritual heirs were than the Sunni sect does. The Shiites also accept and follow a supplemental writing to the Koran, the *Sunna*, which the Sunnis do not. Sunni Muslims base their beliefs on Muhammad's teachings, which were both a religion and a way of organizing society.

Muhammad was born in Mecca in Saudi Arabia. He was the son of a poor shepherd and was orphaned by age six. Muhammad grew up to become a trader, married, and lived a conventional life until the age of 40. In 610 A.D., he had a vision of the Angel Gabriel and felt a special calling from God, or *Allah*. He never claimed to be holy, but said that in his visions the angel told him how Allah wanted the people to live, how they should worship, and what they should believe. He said, "I am only following what has been revealed to me . . . and I give sincere warnings." He warned against the evils of greed and other negative aspects of a society in which the gulf between the rich and the poor was widening. Islam ultimately became a religion of "tolerance and acceptance rather than punishment and vindictiveness," even though some Muslims developed militant tendencies. The Koran defines Islam as a faith of forgiveness that welcomes all people.

Muslims, Christians, and Jews all worship the same God. Many writings in the Koran are similar to those in the Old Testament of the Bible, and the Jewish and Christian prophets are respected in Islam. Muslims believe that Jesus Christ was a great teacher and prophet, but they do not believe he was the Son of God, as Christians do. Muslims also believe that humans will face a final judgment, with heaven waiting for those who have been good and hell waiting for those who have been evil. Muslims also believe in guardian angels.

Not all Libyans embraced Islam at first. The rich did not like Allah's order to share their wealth with the poor, for example. Islam spread through the region quickly, however, through the teachings of Muhammad and his followers and by Arab soldiers who embarked on holy wars. Within 100 years, Islam had spread west to Spain and east to Afghanistan.

In the early 1800s, a man named Sidi Muhammad ibn-Ali as-Sanusi preached the need to return "to the traditional teachings of the Qur'an [Koran] and Muhammad's fundamental beliefs." He sent out teachers to the small communities scattered across the country. Along with teaching the Koran, these men became leaders of these communities, gradually bringing religious law to bear on the whole country.

Libya's History, Culture, Religion, People

Muslims must follow strict rules known as the Five Pillars. The first is a statement of faith, or *Shahada*. "There is no god but Allah; Muhammad is his Prophet." The second Pillar is a strict adherence to daily prayer or *Salat*. Five times every day, Muslims kneel down facing Mecca, and pray. The third Pillar is the requirement to give to the poor, or *Zakat*. The fourth Pillar requires Muslims to fast, or *Sawm*. This is especially important during the ninth month of the Muslim calendar, known as Ramadan. The fifth Pillar requires Muslims to make a pilgrimage to the holy city of Mecca at least once during their lifetime.

Other rules include prohibitions on liquor, gambling, and adultery. Muslims cannot eat pork or other blood meat, cannot charge high interest if they lend money, and in general must be respectful toward people, treating them with honesty, generosity, and fairness—similar to the Golden Rule: Treat others as you would want to be treated.

What's Right With Islam: A New Vision for Muslims and the West, written by Imam Feisal Abdul Rauf of New York, elaborates on how the Western world and the Muslims can bridge their differences and spells out the ways in which America embodies the teachings of Muslim law, or *Shariah*.

Shariah embodies five fundamental rights equal to those outlined in the Declaration of Independence: Muslims believe in the rights to life, freedom of religion, the right to property, family rights, and mental well-being. Rauf compares these to America's "life, liberty, and pursuit of happiness."

GEOGRAPHY

Libya is one of the larger countries in North Africa, with a total of 679,358 square miles (1,759,529 sq km). Its highest elevation is 7,438 feet (2,267 m) above sea level at Beatte Peak or *Bikku Bitti*. Its 1,100 miles (1,770 km) of Mediterranean coastline along its northern edge boasts beautiful sunny beaches and green fields. Tripoli, the capital and main port, is in the northwest and has the highest population density. Most Libyans are Arabs, and Arabic is the country's official language.

Each of Libya's three regions has a unique geography. Tripolitania, which is in the northwest bordering Tunisia and part of Algeria, is mostly sandy flatland with a few lagoons. It covers about 10,000 square miles (25,900 sq km), and the city of Tripoli is located on a major harbor here. The region has agricultural importance and is known for its wheat, barley, watermelons, cauliflower, tomatoes, and groves of date, almond, apricot, fig, olive, and citrus trees. Inland is the long, flat Jafara Plain, which is desert-like and merges into a series of limestone hills, called *Jebel Nefusah*, that reach to 3,000 feet (914 m). Lava rocks and craters indicate that this area was created by volcanoes. Heading south into the Fezzan region, the hills become rocky, red sandstone, which gives the area its nickname: the Red Desert or *Hamadah al-Hamra*.

The Fezzan region, in southwestern Libya, covers more than 212,000 square miles (549,000 sq km). Algeria, Niger, and Chad are adjacent to this region, which is mostly desert with vast, high, shifting sand dunes called *ergs* in Arabic. The rest of the land is made up of rocky and jagged peaks. Dotting the countryside are oases created by underground pools and springs that seep up and are contained in large, bowl-like depressions called *sabkhas*. The oases are vital for traveling herdsmen, and some are even large enough to support small villages or a few families. Along the southern border with Chad, the Tibesti Mountains include Beatte Peak.

The largest region, Cyrenaica, covers nearly half the country. Located along the eastern edge of the country, bordering Egypt and Sudan, it contains fertile soil that supports vineyards and fruit orchards. The port cities of Benghazi, Darnah, and Tobruk are here, as is a large percentage of the population. Tuna are plentiful off its shores. Moving south, the land rises to a height of about 2,900 feet (884 m) to a plateau known as the Green Mountain, or *Al-Jabal al-Akhda*, for the flowers covering its

Libya's History, Culture, Religion, People   29

Libyans shop in the old market in Tripoli. Libya would like to improve its facilities so that foreign tourists could be attracted to the country to visit and spend money.

lower slopes: anemones, cyclamen, lilies, and narcissus. *Al-Kufrah*, one of Libya's largest oases, is located here and was an important stop for the trading caravans that crisscrossed the Sahara, providing food, water, and rest for the nomads. The sheep, goats, and cattle raised in this region provide milk, meat, and hides. Camels raised here are used mainly for transportation.

In Tripoli and Benghazi are small factories that produce processed food, tobacco, salt, fabrics, leather goods, cement, and beverages, as well as materials for the oil industry, including tanks, steel drums, and pipefittings. Besides petroleum, Libya also exports iron ore, salt, gypsum, and sulfur.

FLORA AND FAUNA

For a long time, the only transportation across vast stretches of desert was by camel. Called the "ship of the desert," this animal is well suited for this job and is able to go for many days without water. Introduced to North Africa in the first century by Persian invaders, the camel was a common sight within 100 years. Camels can drink 25 gallons of water at one time, and can store up to 50 gallons within three sections of its stomach. Its hump does not store water, as some think; rather, it stores a large lump of fat that the camel's body relies on when there is no other food or water. During sandstorms, a camel can shut its eyes and nose tightly, almost sealing them, to keep out the blowing particles. The soles of its feet are wide and leathery, making it very surefooted, and enabling the camel to carry up to 1,000 pounds (454 kg) at a time. The camel's milk is good for drinking and for making cheese, and their droppings are dried and used for fuel. Their soft hair is often woven into blankets and tents. For these reasons, and more, early nomads revered their camels. In fact, they believed they would be judged after death based on the kindness they showed to camels.

Besides camels, the desert is home to many other animals, including small rodents, foxes, hyenas, wildcats, and gazelles. Also found in the desert are all kinds of insects, like huge spiders, scorpions, and grasshoppers, and poisonous snakes, like the horned viper, Cleopatra's asp, adders, and kraits. The wadden, a male gazelle, is Libya's national animal and is plentiful along the northern coast.

Few plants can survive in the desert outside of the oases. Scrubby grasses, cactus, and palm trees are plentiful when there is water. The date palm provides fruit, lumber, and fuel, and its fronds are woven into sandals, baskets, and mats. Esparto grass is grown for production of paper and rope, and was once one of Libya's prime exports. The Asphodel lily, an herb, is grown along the coast and is a popular cooking additive. Henna shrubs are used to make dye for the hair and to paint designs on the skin.

For many years, Libya was more or less off-limits to Westerners because of Qaddafi's strong anti-Western sentiments. With recent developments and the beginning of more cordial relations between Libya and the West, tourism is becoming a distinct possibility. Travel restrictions have been lifted, opening up a wealth of opportunities for adventurers. Although hotel accommodations are still improving, those interested in ancient Roman ruins and native settlements will find plenty to do. According to a June 2004 issue of *Time* magazine, tour operators are beginning to lead excursions to the country, which has the "best Roman ruins outside Italy."

CHAPTER

3

Who is Muammar Qaddafi?

The desert outside the city of Sirte, near the northern coastline of Libya, is excruciatingly hot in the summer and extremely cold in the winter. The land is arid, flat, and rocky—a part of the Sahara Desert, which comprises nearly 90 percent of the country. Most people would consider this land uninhabitable. But for the many Bedouins, or nomadic tribes of the desert, it is home.

And it was home for Muammar Qaddafi, who was born there in 1942 or perhaps a few years earlier. The exact date is not documented, but he claims to remember the vicious World War II battles between the Germans and Italians and the allied British and American troops across the deserts of North Africa. These campaigns took place in 1943, however, when Qaddafi would have been too young to remember them. If his claims are true, he may have been born before 1940.

Nomadic Taureg tribesmembers resting with camels in the Sahara desert of Libya, in 2003. Camels were once the sole mode of transportation across the desert; today, they have, for the most part, been replaced by jeeps and other motorized vehicles.

Qaddafi's family was part of a Berber tribe, one of the groups that wandered the desert, making their homes in tents of goat skins stretched over wooden poles. The Berbers were descendants of the inhabitants of the Mediterranean coast before the Arab invasion in the seventh century. His family was part of the Qaddadfa tribe, a small group that lived communally in the ancient tradition of their ancestors, sharing homes, food, and responsibilities. In Arabic, Qaddadfa means "those who spit out or vomit." Although the Qaddadfa were Bedouin Arabs, their bloodlines crisscrossed with those who had inhabited Libya through the centuries, including Turks and Jews.

HIS FAMILY

Qaddafi's father, Mohammed Abdul Salam bin Hamed bin Mohammed, also known as Abu Meniar ("father of the knife") was a camel- and goat-herder who looked after the livestock. Along with a local teacher, he trained Muammar, his youngest child and only son, in the ways of the Koran, the Islamic holy book. Qaddafi's family was fundamentalist Islamic, adhering strictly to the teachings of the prophet Muhammad. They belonged to the Sunni sect of Islam, which is more orthodox and to which most of the world's Muslims belong.

Qaddafi's mother, Aisha, looked after their home, the portable goatskin tent, which was built to keep out the shifting desert sands, and trained her three daughters in the ways of Muslim women. Aisha helped her husband move their home when they migrated with the herds and looked after her family.

Aisha, who died in 1978, and Meniar, who died in 1985, were illiterate, like so many of their generation. But they kept their family's past alive by telling the story of their tribe through stories and songs. Along with this oral history, Qaddafi's parents told their children of the many foreigners who had invaded and occupied their country through the centuries. Qaddafi also learned of the heroes from his country's past, including Sidi Muhammad ibn-Ali as-Sanusi. With his Islamic movement, Sanusi was responsible for giving the diverse tribes of the three provinces, Tripolitania, Cyrenaica, and the Fezzan, a sense of loyalty to a single leader. Through these stories, Qaddafi developed a sense of tribal pride, unwavering religious beliefs, and a strong national identity.

When Muammar was born, Libya was controlled by Italy, the most recent in a long line of foreign occupiers. He grew up hearing the stories of fierce fighting in the early twentieth century. He learned that his grandfather was murdered by an Italian colonist in 1911 and that his father and uncle languished for years as prisoners of war in an Italian jail. Other stories of cruelty and torture were constantly repeated: "Libyans were

Libyan leader Muammar Qaddafi in his father's tent in the Syrtes Desert, Libya. Qaddafi's parents, poor Bedouin, belonged to the Qaddadfa tribe. His father eked out a meager living herding sheep and goats. For years after coming to power, and for unknown reasons, Qaddafi insisted that his parents continue to live in a tent. Despite this, he was close to them throughout their lives.

dropped alive from airplanes; wells were sealed to deprive tribes and their herds of water; livestock were slaughtered . . ." At the end of World War II, with the defeat of the Italians, Britain and France administered Libya. In 1949, the General Assembly of the United Nations called for the establishment of a sovereign Libyan state. Libya was becoming a truly independent country for the first time.

By the time Qaddafi was ten, he was showing an unusual aptitude for learning, language, and especially Islamic teachings. Everyone recognized how bright he was. His father said, " . . . My son is possessed of an unusual intelligence. To educate him will bring blessings from Allah." Fellow tribesmen agreed and helped pay for his early education at an Islamic school in Sirte, where he excelled and was advanced, skipping several grades. From the beginning, Qaddafi was different from most Bedouin boys, who generally did not rise to levels of leadership or national prominence.

During his early teens, Qaddafi spent much time listening to a small transistor radio, a gift from his tribe. It is said that he often would skimp on food in order to buy batteries. He listened to Egyptian radio and the program *Voice of the Arabs*, which was designed to spread Arab nationalism. His sense of political awareness grew through what he heard on the airwaves. Qaddafi later based his plans for overthrowing the monarchy on the Egyptian leader Gamal Abdel Nasser and his speeches, which were broadcast constantly and which Qaddafi listened to almost obsessively. Nasser was a charismatic man, who overthrew King Farouk I in 1952 with the help of the Free Officers' Movement, a group of Egyptian military officers. Nasser formed an Arab republic, becoming premier in 1954. He put much needed political and economic changes into place.

Qaddafi embraced Nasser's philosophies, including his calls for Arab unity and the rejection of Western ties. Nasser encouraged a sense of nationalism among his countrymen and sought to lessen foreign influence, while encouraging Arab-speaking countries, including Libya, Tunisia, Morocco, Syria, Lebanon, Iraq, Jordan, Saudi Arabia, and Yemen, to pull together with Egypt. A friend of Qaddafi's from that time remembered, "We used to make jokes about how if he thought so highly of Nasser, he should become an Egyptian."

Nasser's speeches were electrifying. His appeals for Arab unity centered on the common religion of Islam and the common hatred of Israel, which had been established less than a decade earlier. According to Nasser, the land on which the Israelis lived was stolen from the Palestinians, their Arab brothers. He asserted that Israel was not established to create a homeland for Jews, as the West claimed, but to provide Western nations with a country that would be beholden to them and give them a foothold among Arab nations.

If these speeches held the average Arab spellbound, their effect on Qaddafi was even more pronounced. He felt a psychic connection with the Egyptian leader: They both believed strongly in Arab unity; they both practiced and encouraged strict adherence to the Koran and Islamic tradition; they both mistrusted and hated foreigners, especially Westerners; and they were both strongly nationalistic, planning for the betterment of their countries.

ROOTS OF THE REVOLUTION

Even at this young age, Qaddafi began to form a plan to bring Nasser's belief system to his country, with himself as the leader of a new Libya.

The same year that Libya gained its independence, Qaddafi graduated from the school in Sirte, and was sent to the Sebha preparatory school in Fezzan, where he made friends and formed cliques that would later became revolutionary groups. Many of these boy became part of the corps that overthrew King Idris I in 1969. Many cells were formed and although members of the individual groups did not know one another, Qaddafi knew them all. The way this worked was that each cell had four boys as members. Each boy would then go out and recruit three others, forming a second cell. Each of these new boys would do the same, and so on. So each student knew only about two cells, the one to which he first belonged, and the one he formed.

Qaddafi's charisma and sense of purpose were intoxicating to the other students eager for change. He was focused and decisive and able to sway others easily to his point of view. He inspired trust in those who joined him, and they followed his orders absolutely.

Qaddafi's activism became more pronounced, and he organized marches that were pro-Egypt and anti-Israel and

In this 1956 photo, Egyptian Premier Gamal Abdel Nasser shakes hands with King Idris I of Libya. Nasser had been trying to win the position of spokesperson for the Arab nations in North Africa, as well as the Near East. Nasser strongly influenced Qaddafi's political ideology and possibly his decision to eventually wrest power from King Idris.

gave inflammatory speeches that drew the attention of the police and his school's administration. He was expelled from Sebha in 1961 for his "treasonable behavior." His schooling soon continued at the University of Libya, where he studied history, political science, Marxism, and Communism. He also studied military training, and he encouraged his classmates to do the same. Many of these boys later became officers in the Libyan Army. He graduated from the university, earning high grades and a law degree. He chose not to practice law, and instead attended the Benghazi Military Academy, where he was accepted because of his stellar academic achievements in spite of his past incendiary behavior.

Many students at the academy came from rich families with ties to the king or were sons of businessmen who dealt with foreign companies. They were not serious students or soldiers, but playboys who gambled, drank, and ran around with women—all activities forbidden by fundamentalist Muslim teachings. Qaddafi had nothing to do with these students, who he felt were corrupted by Western influences. Instead, he again formed a group of friends, soldiers who had similar backgrounds and held similar beliefs. Most came from poor families and were more comfortable in the desert than the city. They retained strong tribal ties and were devout Muslims. They did not drink alcohol or smoke, gamble or go dancing. They remained virgins until after marriage, prayed, studied, and planned with Qaddafi for the revolution to come.

After graduating from the academy, Qaddafi, who was commissioned as a lieutenant in the Libyan Army, was sent to England for six months for advanced signal corps training and to develop communications systems. He called the English lifestyle "godless and decadent" and felt that Americans were simply a variation on the British. After his return to Libya in 1966, he spent a lot of time planning the overthrow of King Idris, eventually recruiting about 7,000 members of the army to support the coup. The recruits held secret meetings and continued to enlist new members. Despite their large and growing membership, they remained undiscovered by the thousands of the king's secret police.

Muammar Qaddafi was recognized as "special" by his family, fellow villagers, and later his classmates. His dark eyes and penetrating gaze commanded attention. His intelligence inspired awe. His temperament has been described as arrogant and mercurial, and he also was known to be quite stubborn and willful. As he grew, these qualities only intensified. It is said that he is paranoid and easily depressed, but somehow through all these extreme personality traits, Muammar Qaddafi has managed to rule Libya for more than 35 years.

CHAPTER

4

Government— Qaddafi's Way

The groups of boys whom Qaddafi had led as children had grown up along with him. Many remained his loyal supporters in the Army and belonged to a group called the Free Officers' Movement. They swore to follow him in pursuit of his dream of creating a pan-Arab state, beginning with the overthrow of the Libyan monarchy.

Late in the night of September 1, 1969, during what was supposedly a training exercise, Qaddafi's troops raided the palace of King Idris I while he was in Turkey. They occupied Tripoli, Benghazi, and small towns across the country. Qaddafi's men took over the radio station in Benghazi, virtually the only source of information for much of Libya. In a short time, Libyans, from city dwellers to desert nomads listening on their transistor radios, heard about the overthrow of "the reactionary, backward, and decadent regime" of the king. The voice on the radio spoke of the new government, the Libyan Arab Republic, and encouraged everyone to join against the "enemy of Islam." Everyone listening knew this meant Israel.

That voice on the radio belonged to Colonel Muammar Qaddafi, who had promoted himself from captain as soon as the coup proved successful. Qaddafi made it clear from the start that this new government would be independent and not the "pawn" of foreign powers. He announced, "From now on, Libya is deemed a free, sovereign republic under the name of the Libyan Arab Republic, ascending with God's help to exalted heights." He included a call for Libyans to "stand together against the enemy of the Arab nation, the enemy of Islam, the enemy of humanity who destroyed our holy places and shattered our honor." He ended with, "O you who witnessed the holy war, who fought the good fight . . . O sons of the steppes, sons of the ancient cities, the upright countryside. O sons of the villages . . . the hour of work has come. Forward." Within hours, he had summoned U.S., French, and Soviet diplomats and explained what had happened and how his new government would be run.

No one, including Egypt's Nasser or other Arab leaders, really knew who Qaddafi was. They did know they were nervous that the king had been so easily overthrown. And as it turned out, what they thought they knew about Qaddafi in the beginning was later proven to be terribly wrong. The United States originally supported the regime change, primarily because of Qaddafi's anti-Communist stance, and even provided CIA protection. Although Britain's treaty with Libya called for protection in case of a threat to the monarchy, Britain did not adhere to its agreement. Idris's nephew, Crown Prince Hassan Rida, declined to take over the throne, and instead, urged Libyans to support Qaddafi's regime.

At the time of the coup, King Idris was 79 years old and in failing health. Because he was childless, he had appointed Hassan Rida as heir. Before the coup, rumors spread that Rida

Government—Qaddafi's Way

Libyan students remove a portrait of deposed King Idris I at their country's embassy in Damascus, Syria, in September 1969, in reaction to Qaddafi's successful coup in Libya. The students took over the embassy, forcing diplomats to flee.

was plotting to kill Idris and take over the throne. Whether this is true is unknown. Regardless, Idris approved a counterplan to kill Rida. Idris's top generals developed this plot and had planned to take over the government themselves after Idris's death. They knew Qaddafi, who many felt was the most promising young officer in the army. When the generals tempted Qaddafi with the offer of an important role in their new government, he agreed to lend his support. But he was really only stalling them, trying to buy a little more time to strengthen his secret group of supporters and soldiers, and to perfect his plan to overthrow the king himself.

Within three months of the coup, the CIA was approached by two of Qaddafi's generals who were upset by his methods. They outlined a plot to overthrow Qaddafi and return the monarchy to Rida. Because the United States was worried that Qaddafi would sell oil to the Soviets and not to them, the CIA warned Qaddafi, who stopped the plotters in their tracks.

Qaddafi was named prime minister of the Socialist Libyan Arab Republic. He also was appointed head of the armed forces. Qaddafi believed that governmental authority should be spread throughout the people, so he set up the government with multiple layers. According to Terri Willis's book, *Libya: Enchantment of the World*, "Qaddafi based his plans on three factors: economic and political freedom for the people; unity throughout Libya and with other nations in the Arab world; and the use of Islamic law as the overall guide for justice." He called this system direct democracy, because in theory every citizen has a say in the way the country is run.

Qaddafi established a twelve-man ruling authority called the Revolutionary Command Council (RCC) with himself as chairman. The original constitution called Libya "an Arab democratic and free republic which constitutes a part of the Arab nation and whose objective is comprehensive Arab unity."

Qaddafi's new government was a blend of socialism, nationalism, and Islam, or what he called "Islamic Socialism." He was an avid reader of theories of government, as well as a scholar of the Koran, and he developed this form of government from his readings. When Qaddafi declared the Koran to be the basis of his new regime, the leaders of the Sunni Muslims were not happy because of the inclusion of Socialist doctrine.

Government—Qaddafi's Way

Muammar Qaddafi speaks to demonstrators gathered to show their support for his return after he resigned as leader of the Revolutionary Command Council. The council refused to accept Qaddafi's resignation, and he eventually agreed to be reinstated.

They believed Socialism to be godless and held Qaddafi responsible for desecrating their culture through his attempt to fuse the two beliefs.

THE GREEN BOOK

Qaddafi recorded his theories in 1976 in a three-volume book titled *The Green Book*. Green is the color of Islam and of Libya's flag. Within its pages, he outlined his views of government, economics, religion, and cultural rights and wrongs. He believed he had written out the perfect political system, which he called the Third Universal Theory. He wrote that the goal of "New Socialism" was "to create a society that is happy because it is free." He felt that the people of Libya should be able to meet their spiritual and material needs without control from an outside government.

Qaddafi wrote that capitalism and Communism were "repugnant" and believed his theory was a better alternative. He wrote that *The Green Book* "presents the ultimate solution to the problem of the instrument of government." Libya's new constitution was based solely on the *Shariah*. According to Islam, the Shariah governs all aspects of a person's life. It provides strict punishments for every infringement. For example, if someone were to break the fast of Ramadan, the Muslims' month-long fast where nothing is eaten during daylight hours, he could be whipped. If someone committed armed robbery, he might lose an arm or a foot.

The Koran calls for religious tolerance and respect for those who worship differently than Muslims. Qaddafi broke from these laws through his persecution of Jews and Christians in the early days of his regime. He forced Jews to leave Libya and seized their property. Most Christian churches were shut down. Although he stopped persecuting these two groups as stringently, the effects are still felt by the minority of those who follow a religion other than Islam. Qaddafi has allowed Jewish synagogues and schools to be rebuilt in Tripoli as a sign of his tolerance.

In *The Green Book* Qaddafi wrote negatively about amassing personal wealth. He wrote that large sums of money were saved only at the expense of others, and that no person should save more than was needed. "Any surplus beyond the satisfaction of needs should ultimately belong to all members of society. Those who acquire excessively are undoubtedly thieves." In the early years, Qaddafi tried to get people to give up their savings voluntarily, but many simply hid their money. In the 1980s,

Qaddafi changed Libya's currency, requiring people to exchange their money for the new bills. The catch was that the government would only exchange the equivalent of $2,100 in U.S. dollars. Anything more was held by the government, and a receipt—which was later useless—was given. The extra funds were used to provide social services to the poor. Those who lost much money were angry with Qaddafi and were not motivated to work harder to earn more, taking a toll on Libya's economy.

Some of Qaddafi's ideas have shifted over the years, including his early beliefs about women. In *The Green Book* he wrote, " . . . Woman is but a female with a biological nature different from that of man. . . . Man and woman cannot be equal. . . . Education that leads to work unsuitable for her nature is unjust and cruel as well." In later years, however, Qaddafi allowed women to attend universities and opened the military draft to women. An all-female personal guard, outfitted with red berets and machine guns, acts as his security contingent when he appears in public.

He also wrote about women: " . . . Motherhood is the female's function. . . . While man is strong and tough because he is created in that way, woman is gentle not because she wanted to be, but because she is created so. There is no absolute equality between men and women." He felt that as long as women continued to be good mothers and wives, first and foremost, then they had the right and duty to participate in the country's economy. But in opening up education to women, Qaddafi changed female roles in Libya forever. To attend universities, women have moved to cities in greater numbers, where they experience freedoms never before imagined. Education created literate women—women who were as literate as the men of their generation and more literate than their fathers. Fundamentalist Muslims denounced free college education because of the belief that an educated woman would not be a good wife or mother. Many Libyan women wear Western-style dress, do not veil their faces, and work at jobs

A group of young cadets at the women's military academy in Tripoli cheer during their graduation, attended by Libyan chief of state Muammar Qaddafi. The academy opened in 1979 during Qaddafi's push to include women in Libya's armed forces, against fundamentalist Islamic law and much resistance.

previously held only by men, all reasons that fundamentalist Islamic leaders do not like Qaddafi.

As for the workplace, Qaddafi declared that all workers should become partners in the place where they work. Rather than being paid by a boss, each worker would co-own the business and split any profits equally. He wrote: "Wage-earners are but slaves to the masters who hire them. In this society, there are no wage-earners, but partners." Predictably, this notion of the efficient workplace was flawed. Business came almost to a standstill since it was nearly impossible to make business decisions when everyone had a say. The government added layers of red tape in the form of additional rules and regulations, but before long Qaddafi recognized his mistake and relaxed many regulations, allowing some businesses to be owned individually.

A VOICE TO THE MASSES

In his attempt to give every citizen a voice, he renamed the country in 1977. Libya became the Socialist People's Libyan Arab Jamahiriya, indicating a republic of the masses. True democracy would require every citizen to vote on every issue, which Qaddafi realized was too cumbersome and impossible to accomplish. So he established small governmental bodies within twenty-four municipalities, broken up into 186 zones. Adults over age 18 vote for members of their local Basic People's Congress. These representatives serve in the General People's Congress, consisting of more than 1,000 members. This group reports to Qaddafi, who is called the Revolutionary Leader. Serving just below Qaddafi is the five-member General Secretariat, (formerly the Revolutionary Command Council), which is supported by the sixteen-member General People's Committee. In reality, although individuals have a voice, Qaddafi remains the final authority, supported by a military force ready and willing to take on any challengers. Only one political party is allowed, and it controls the economy.

Qaddafi's leadership was inconsistent. He called himself "Brother Colonel," declaring that he was equal to all the people. He even tried to establish an image of himself as a simple man: His family lived in a tent, and he used another tent for an office; he drank camel's milk and ate homemade Berber bread. But he was not "just another Libyan"—he was in total command. He strictly enforced the laws of Shariah, including closing any places that sold alcohol or offered gambling or dancing. Once he led a raid on a Tripoli nightclub, marched onto stage in his uniform, fired his gun at the ceiling several times and announced: "This sinkhole of Western depravity is now officially closed!"

But he did not always follow Shariah himself. Several months after the coup, Qaddafi, then 27, married Fathia Nouri Khaled in an arranged marriage. She was the daughter of an Army general, one of the king's officers. Nasser attended the wedding. Contrary to Muslim law, the bride was already pregnant and delivered a son several months after the wedding. Soon after the birth, the two were divorced. Many of Qaddafi's followers disapproved of the divorce, especially after it was discovered that he had been having an affair with a nurse who cared for him while he recuperated from an appendectomy less than two weeks after the wedding. Qaddafi married the nurse, Sifiiya, and they went on to have six children.

Predictably, those who lived in the cities and were most affected by the new restrictive laws did not like them; those in the countryside supported them. To find out who was with him and who was against him, Qaddafi would sometimes disguise himself as a herdsman and go out among the Berbers. In his conversations with these men, he found support. When he dressed as someone from the city and went into the streets, he heard complaints about the new laws and rising unemployment. Along with the ban on dancing and drinking alcohol, certain books were outlawed, and the Koran became the most popular book. Media outlets became government-controlled, and Qaddafi's critics and opponents were arrested or exiled.

Qaddafi encouraged a population shift in Libya after 1969. He wanted rural citizens to move to the cities so it would be easier to provide them education and health care and to organize them into political groups. Unfortunately, this move separated the people from their traditional way of life. The chain of authority of tribal leaders was broken, and Qaddafi's government gained more control. Today more than 75 percent of Libyans live in urban areas.

Over the years Qaddafi has been embraced and revered, but as time passed, his popularity decreased—mainly because of his foreign aggression and his financial and training support of anti-American terrorists. This extremism drained the Libyan economy, and everyone felt its impact. Also, many Libyans resent the numerous military conflicts and the resulting deaths. And they do not like the draft, especially of women. Libya's overall militarization, coupled with the arrogance of many of Qaddafi's officers, breeds resentment, which has caused a backlash against his government and a return to fundamentalist Islamic roots.

When Qaddafi took over the country, the lives of most regular citizens did improve because he redirected the large sums of money that flowed in as petroleum flowed out. This money was used to improve the country's infrastructure. Some of his countrymen resent Qaddafi because he refuses to accept differing opinions and he isn't open to new ideas. As with most leaders, he is loved by some and hated by others.

CHAPTER

5

Oil and Water: A Potent Economic Combination for Libya

Millions of years ago the Sahara Desert, the world's largest, was covered with lush, verdant vegetation and dotted with lakes. Cave paintings left behind prove the land was inhabited. By Roman times, the climate had changed, and the vast sandy region that we are familiar with today had formed over the ancient rock. This land would become Libya.

No rivers run through the Sahara, but *wadis*, or dry gulches that fill with rainwater, appear from time to time. They dry out quickly, however, from the heat of the sun. Underground springs bubble up in desert oases, providing needed shade and drinking water for the nomads who still cross the desert and the tribes who call the larger oases their home. Salt lakes, or *sebkhas*, are found closer to the Mediterranean Sea.

Before the discovery of oil deep underground in the Sahara

Oil and Water: A Potent Economic Combination for Libya

Desert in 1959, Libya was one of the world's poorest countries; after its discovery, it became one of the wealthiest. Beforehand, the people sustained themselves mainly by hunting and gathering what they could as they wandered the desert with their livestock. Some sold crafts in the villages, and a few rudimentary industries existed. Those who traded goods across the desert did so at their peril as the heat, the lack of water, and thieves who preyed on traders made this a dangerous undertaking. The country depended in large part on financial aid from the United States and Great Britain.

American and British geologists and engineers believed that oil existed under the Sahara, and they worked for more than twenty years to prove their theories. Their exploration was dangerous because hundreds of buried land mines from World War II remained. Sudden sandstorms also made for slow going, covering the men and their equipment with a gritty, dirty coating.

A spot in the desert called Jebel Zelten was thought to contain an oil reserve. The Esso Oil Company, now known as Exxon, drilled the "lucky well." Once oil began to flow there, the well produced 15,000 barrels a day, exceptional by any standard. This first Libyan well produced much more than those in Iran, which was considered oil-rich with wells getting about 5,300 barrels a day each. Also, Libya's oil is considered high quality because it has a low sulfur content, which makes it cleaner than oil from most other countries in the region and cheaper to refine into gasoline. Today, Libyan oil fields can be found within a 600-by-300-mile (965-by-483-km) swath across the desert.

The discovery of oil totally changed the Libyan way of life by creating jobs and increasing wages. Before oil was found, Libyan workers earned an average of $25 to $50 (U.S.) a year. By the mid-1960s, income increased to an average of $1,500 a year. Qaddafi's goal was to improve the country's overall infrastructure using income from oil; something Idris had not done.

Esso Standard Libya Inc., a storage facility at the refinery and pipeline terminal of the Zelten and Raguba oil fields, at Marsa El Brega, Libya, 1955. Qaddafi used the wealth generated by the Libyan oil industry, in general, to improve living conditions for the Libyan people.

Instead, the king had lined his own pockets and those of his friends and family. Qaddafi allowed foreign oil companies to drill wells and taxed them, using the revenue to build modern housing with indoor plumbing, hospitals, schools, and roads.

He also used some of this money to build irrigation systems in the desert to improve agriculture. Once crops were sustained by the irrigation systems, they were used at home and for export.

Gradually, Qaddafi took back many of the oil fields from their international operators and nationalized them, making them government property. Then he rented the fields back to the foreigners, using this rental income for further popular reforms. These reforms in education, housing, transportation, and health care dramatically improved the lives of the average Libyan for a time.

In the last year of King Idris I's reign, in 1969, only $5 million was budgeted for the school system. By 1978, $75 million was set aside annually to educate the country's children. Also in 1969, only 80,000 girls and 185,000 boys attended elementary school, but by 1978, 285,000 girls and 315,000 boys were in grade school. About one-third of Libya's population was of school age at this time, and the literacy rate began to rise.

Improved health care included medical and dental care, and free hospitalization and prescription drugs. Community clinics opened to serve citizens in the cities as well as in rural outposts. Disease prevention and inoculation programs were key in improving the people's health. Rabies, once a big problem in the desert, was nearly eradicated, as was leprosy. Libyan children were vaccinated against polio, measles, smallpox, and more.

The government made improved housing a priority as well. Most new homes were built with indoor bathrooms, kitchens, and electricity. As new housing developments went up, the cities reflected an interesting mix of architecture, as modern apartment buildings coexisted with ancient structures.

Overall, the standard of living rose dramatically. Thousands of jobs were created in the oil industry, and in factories that manufactured products, like televisions, cars, and refrigerators, that were desired by the newly well off. People also found jobs in shops selling these items. After a time, however, with

Qaddafi's increased support of terrorism and the imposition of trade and economic sanctions, the Libyans' quality of life began a downward spiral. War, farm failures, food shortages, and a breakdown in industry and transportation were the downside. But it is arguable that the people in general were better under Qaddafi's rule and his management of oil income than they were under King Idris.

DEMANDS ON FOREIGN COMPANIES

Even though the influx of oil money helped the Libyan economy overall, the instability of oil prices over the decades has had a negative impact. International embargoes and regulation by OPEC, the Organization of Petroleum Exporting Countries, have limited oil revenues and hurt the Libyans. OPEC is a cartel of oil-producing nations that agree on the quantity and prices of exported oil. Oil is the root of Libya's economy, sometimes to the detriment of other exports. For example, the transportation of oil for export sometimes takes precedence over the transportation of crops, leaving some to wither and die in the fields. The crops that do get to the market are often few and of poor quality. A lack of supply then causes prices to rise.

In 1970 Qaddafi put pressure on the foreign oil companies in Libya, insisting that the price of Libyan crude oil be raised sharply to finance some of his development projects. Some companies gave in to his demands, which worried the United States. The Americans were concerned that other OPEC nations would follow his lead, leading to high gasoline prices and worldwide shortages.

Larger companies, like Exxon, could afford to ignore Qaddafi's demands, but some smaller companies, including Occidental Petroleum, a mid-sized California company, required the Libyan reserves to stay in business. According to Douglas Little in his book, *American Orientalism: The United States and the Middle East Since 1945*, Qaddafi was well aware of the precarious economic conditions of some of these companies. He warned Occidental's owner, Armand Hammer, that "unless the firm hiked prices by 15 percent and increased Libya's share of the profits to 55 percent, its concession would be revoked." Occidental refused at first, and Qaddafi responded by cutting back on Libyan oil, creating shortages in Western Europe in the early summer of 1970.

Occidental eventually gave in to Qaddafi's demands after it was unable to identify a secondary source of petroleum and after Exxon refused to guarantee Occidental enough crude oil to offset its losses. U.S. officials and oil executives saw Occidental's agreement with Qaddafi as potentially dangerous. Like a game of dominoes where tiles continue to fall once the first one is knocked over, Occidental was seen as the first tile to go down. Agreements by one company to Qaddafi's demands could be used against another company and so on until Libya controlled each oil company operating there.

By early 1971, Qaddafi had forced oil companies to raise the price of Libyan crude oil by 90 cents per barrel and to give Libya 60 percent of their profits. Compliance by the oil companies had exactly the expected result. Other OPEC members chimed in, demanding higher prices for their crude and a larger cut of the profits.

Little wrote: "By early 1973, some State Department officials worried that America's deepening dependence on Middle Eastern crude, OPEC's mounting leverage over the multinationals, and growing Arab frustration with Washington's special relationship with Israel could easily trigger an oil crisis." By this time, the United States's reliance on Middle Eastern oil had greatly increased. For anyone who lived in the early 1970s, long lines at gas stations and rationing are unwelcome memories.

As for Libya's oil deposits today: Some predict that underground supplies will be depleted by 2015. What will Libya turn to then to finance education, its health care system, and other social programs?

WATER: ANOTHER VALUABLE RESOURCE

Lack of water has long plagued Libya, with its vast expanse of desert and no freshwater lakes. Large aquifers exist deep below the surface and have supplied the country with drinking water for years. Thousands of years ago, when the climate of North Africa was moderate and more rain fell each year, excess rainwater would seep through the porous sandstone, becoming trapped underground and forming the huge aquifers. Along with desalination plants by the Mediterranean Sea, these aquifers were the only source of water for humans and their herds, and for the irrigation of crops. Unfortunately, the water that came from these plants or the aquifers close to the coast was not always of the best quality for drinking or irrigation.

During oil exploration in the late 1950s and early 1960s in the southern Libyan desert, vast reservoirs of underground water were discovered. Four underground basins have been found, and Libya hopes they will provide water for the country for many years to come.

Studies were done on the viability of creating a new agricultural center near these underground pools. But rather than relocate the majority of the population from the coast, south toward the border with Chad where the water was found, the government decided to bring the water to the people via a series of pipelines.

In October 1983, the Great Man-Made River Project was begun. A governing authority was established and given the responsibility of moving water from the southern aquifers to the population centers and profitable farms of the north. This undertaking is about half completed, with water being delivered to homes and fields in and around Tripoli. The pipelines carry more than five million cubic meters of water each day from the desert to the coast. The additional crops grown through this irrigation are used at home and for export.

The cost of this project has been huge, more than $25 billion.

Oil and Water: A Potent Economic Combination for Libya

A crowd wades in flowing water during a nighttime celebration marking the opening of Salluq Reservoir, one of Qaddafi's biggest manmade river projects. Such projects, begun in 1983, aimed to bring water from the southern aquifers to the farms and cities of the northern coastline.

Pipes run for 2,500 miles (4,000 km) underground, transferring water from hundreds of wells into reservoirs that feed the network. Unfortunately, a lot of water evaporates from these reservoirs. But the project has supplied water for home, industrial, and agricultural use. Farm co-ops have been established, and irrigation equipment, electricity, and well pumps have been supplied to people living in the desert. In terms of improving Libya's self-sufficiency and reducing its dependence on foreign food imports, the project seems to be a success.

But it has had its critics, mainly because of the high cost and its inefficiency. Some call it the "Great Mad Man River Project" and claim it would have made more sense to build more desalination plants along the Mediterranean. From the beginning, some scientists predicted that removing this much water from under the desert would cause massive cave-ins, and damage the surface. They said, too, that the wells would be drained within 50 years. Others thought it would be cheaper to import food. But the project's supporters—including, of course, the government that came up with the idea—insisted that its benefits would outweigh the damages. Thousands of new jobs were just one of the benefits cited.

Concerns were raised during the construction of the Great Man-Made River: Was it really a way to hide military equipment and troops? The tunnels, after all, were so large—seemingly much larger than needed to transport only water. This theory has not been proved.

CHAPTER

6

Never-ending Battles with the Rest of the World

When Qaddafi and his troops overthrew King Idris, they arrested 600 army officers, politicians, businessmen, and government officials. The Roman Catholic Cathedral of the Sacred Heart of Jesus was converted into the Mosque of Gamal Abdel Nasser, and Arabic replaced English everywhere. Qaddafi announced that the "revolution was for President Nasser" of Egypt, his role model. He also said, "Nasser can take everything of ours and add it to the rest of the Arab world's resources to be used for battle."

These statements and actions emphasized Qaddafi's extreme pan-Arabism and intolerance of other beliefs. Those close to him have called him moody, impulsive, and unpredictable, with a fiery

Former Egyptian President Gamal Abdel Nasser, shown in a September 1966 photograph. To the West, Nasser was a dangerous radical. To most Arabs, he was a hero who fought three wars with Israel and would never accept the existence of the Jewish state. Many, however, thought that Nasser actively sought peace with Israel but was rejected by Israeli leaders.

temper. His speeches reiterated his belief that the use of violence is an effective means to an end. His protection and sponsorship of international terrorists continued in the face of widespread international pressure, even from other Arab nations.

Qaddafi's childhood was filled with stories of occupation, terror, and torture of his people and of Libya's domination by other countries over the centuries. Through these tales Qaddafi formed his attitudes toward the rest of the world. He felt that anyone who was not an Arab or a Muslim was wrong. Though as a child and a young man, Qaddafi tended to be pragmatic, he was known to also have a recklessness that seems to have continued into adulthood. Many of his actions have been coldly calculated, but also come across as somewhat desperate.

Qaddafi took these pro-Arabic/pro-Islamic beliefs to the extreme. He provided land for terrorist training camps. He gave cover to those operatives who were later convicted of bombing a West Berlin nightclub and to those who conspired to down Pan Am Flight 103 over Lockerbie, Scotland. He consented to the production and use of poison gas and other deadly chemicals. He also spent millions of dollars, maybe billions, to ensure that Libya would never again be occupied by a foreign power. He amassed so much equipment and so many guns that his country has a large surplus of military supplies.

Qaddafi's overspending on the military and his eager use of his military equipment has led to repercussions. In the 1980s, the United States had several opportunities to retaliate against Qaddafi for his attacks against American citizens as well as actions against other countries. Trade sanctions were imposed first by the United States; other sanctions came later from the United Nations, including a ban against incoming and outgoing international flights and a limit on the sale and purchase of equipment used in the oil industry. These sanctions caused widespread damage to the oil industry specifically and to the overall economy in general.

As long as Qaddafi has been in control, Libya has been involved in wars and various conflicts with most of its neighbors. Qaddafi has led Libya into conflicts with Egypt, Tunisia, and Chad. He rejected any peace process between Israel and Palestine. Through his support of terrorism and his refusal to move with the times in the peacemaking process, he became a pariah even among leaders who might otherwise consider him more of an ally than an enemy. Many neighbors, along with most of the world, considered him a leader of a rogue nation.

In his 1998 book, *Rogue Regimes: Terrorism and Proliferation*, Raymond Tanter wrote that Libya should definitely be included on the list of rogue nations because of its large conventional military force, its support of international terrorism, and its production of weapons of mass destruction. He also included Libya because the State Department added it to a list called "Patterns of Global Terrorism," which is released annually by the Office of the Coordinator for Counterterrorism.

In discussing leaders like Qaddafi, Fidel Castro of Cuba, Saddam Hussein of Iraq, and Kim Jong Il of North Korea, Tanter wrote: "As these men go about the unsavory business of terrorism and acquiring weapons of mass destruction, the world has a choice: to contain, embrace, or pursue a mixed policy toward these outlaw regimes. The new international villains are leaders of nations that have large conventional military forces and that condone international terrorism and/or seek weapons of mass destruction, including nuclear, biological, and chemical armaments."

Qaddafi fits the visual image most people have of a "rogue" leader. The stereotype is of a stern, almost angry looking man wearing a military uniform and dark glasses, carrying himself with an imposing demeanor. Tanter even compared Qaddafi to a "rogue elephant" that wanders from its herd, meaning he does not follow the ways of his group, but takes independent actions that might alienate and anger the others.

Qaddafi and the other leaders mentioned by Tanter had the opportunity to establish their regimes more or less unnoticed by the rest of the world. While the United States and the Soviet Union were deeply involved in the Cold War, and the Western world looked on anxiously, these leaders were able to set up the type of governments that worked for them, and make moves with little notice.

"Without the checks and balances of a democratic system or the constraints of large-scale bureaucracies, rogue regimes are subject to the whims of charismatic individuals . . . holding the future of international stability in their hands," Tanter wrote.

These countries have provided a dilemma for the European Union and the United States because their leaders are intent on pursuing their own agendas for nuclear proliferation, development of weapons of mass destruction, and power plays against their neighbors or other countries. Both the United States and the European Union rely on Libya for oil, but refuse to allow it to continue in its rebellious ways. For the United States, there can be no gray area where Qaddafi is concerned. The United States holds a black/white, either/or viewpoint, which has led in the past to an imposition of threats and coercion to try to control him.

The Europeans, on the other hand, take in the good and the bad, creating a multilateral system for dealing with the world. Tanter called the United States idealistic and the European Union realistic. He says the Europeans wonder why the United States believes it has the right to impose its moral authority on other countries and do not understand how the United States believes that negative actions can have positive reactions.

AGGRESSION AGAINST NEIGHBORS

After Abdel Nasser's death on Sept. 28, 1970, Qaddafi tried to become the leader of several Arab states, following Nasser's belief in Arab nationalism. In 1972, he proclaimed the Federation of Arab Republics to include Libya, Egypt, and Syria. The agreement outlined a merger, which was to take place by September 1, 1973, naming Egyptian President Anwar Sadat as the federation's president, and Qaddafi as vice president and head of the military. Although it sounded promising in theory, the attempt was derailed when Sadat and Qaddafi could not agree on specific terms of the merger. By the end

Anwar Sadat (seated, left), Muammar Qaddafi (seated, center), and Hafez Assad (seated, right), the leaders of Egypt, Libya, and Syria, respectively, sign an agreement in April 1971 establishing the "Federation of Arab Republics." The agreement had no lasting impact.

of the decade, neither Egypt, Tunisia or Chad—all Libya's neighbors—wanted anything to do with Qaddafi because of his encouragement of terrorist groups that might have wanted to overthrow their governments.

During the late 1970s, Qaddafi invaded its neighbor to the east, Sudan, which also shares a border with Egypt. This invasion frightened Sadat, who felt that Egypt could be next on Qaddafi's list. He also feared that if Libyan forces, backed by the Soviets, conquered Sudan, these extremists would control the Nile River, where many of Egypt's citizens work. Because of these fears, Sadat approached Jimmy Carter, then the U.S. president, for help against Qaddafi. Sadat proposed a buildup of his military flanks, with Carter's help, to "deter and confront Libyan aggression." Carter declined any assistance, causing Sadat to question Carter's commitment to Egypt.

General Ariel Sharon of Israel joined Sadat in condemning Libya in 1981, because of his belief that Qaddafi posed a serious threat to his country. Sharon's fears about Qaddafi and the failing relationship between Libya and Egypt were based on Qaddafi's financial and political support of the Palestine Liberation Organization (PLO) in the late 1970s. Qaddafi disagreed with the peace agreement that Egypt pursued with Israel in 1979, and his worsening relationship with Egypt led Qaddafi to approach the Soviet Union for support. Libya bought high-tech Russian military supplies, including the supersonic MiG-25 combat fighters.

RELATIONS WITH THE UNITED STATES

By 1981, the Reagan administration was convinced that the Soviet Union was trying to undermine any effort at cooperation between Washington and Libya because of the arms it was selling to Libya. Yemen and Ethiopia, which had an informal alliance with Libya, were essentially also being supplied with weapons through the sale of Soviet guns to Libya. The Soviet Union's support of Libya also ensured that it would have access to Libyan oil as well as to Tripoli and other points along Libya's coast. "Reagan officials not only believed that the U.S. had a strategic interest in arresting Soviet inroads into the Middle East, but were prepared to combine economic diplomacy with military force to achieve that objective in the case of Libya," Tanter wrote.

Because of Libya's alignment with the Soviet Union, the Reagan administration simply could not stand by and ignore Libya's actions during the 1980s. It, too, was troubled by Libya's beliefs about Palestinian independence, its support of Iran in the Iran–Iraq war of 1980 to 1988, and its support of various "independence movements" around the world. Relations between the West and Libya grew increasingly strained during the Reagan years. Someone in this administration was credited with labeling Qaddafi "the most dangerous man in the world." In March 1982, Libyan oil imports were banned in the United States.

At the end of the 1980s, three events occurred, prompting the United States to convene an international conference in Paris: Libya built a poison gas facility at Rabta; Iran and Iraq used chemical weapons during their war, with deadly results; and Saddam Hussein killed thousands of his own Kurdish countrymen with poison gas. This was the first time the world became aware of the dangerous proliferation of chemical and biological weapons.

The main goal of the Paris Conference was to encourage the countries that had signed the 1925 Geneva Protocol to restate their commitment to that document. The signers of that agreement promised not to use "asphyxiating, poisonous, or other gases, analogous liquids, materials, or devices, in wartime." A second objective was to discourage the use of chemical weapons in the world. Washington hoped to get a treaty signed to prohibit the production and storage of these weapons, and one to implement economic sanctions against any country using chemical weapons.

At the conference, Qaddafi, who attended because Libya had signed the 1925 pact, tried to convince other attendees that he was against the production and use of chemical weapons. He suggested that chemical plants in America, Europe, and Israel posed more danger to the world. To the American charges that he was building a chemical plant, Qaddafi replied that the facility was used only to produce pharmaceuticals.

CLOSER TO HOME

Qaddafi's disregard for human life and for international cooperation took its toll at home as well as abroad. From 1975 to 1981, opposition to the leader grew within Libya. He survived at least six coup attempts by groups that had plotted in exile. In

February 1980, he responded to these threats by authorizing the "physical liquidation of enemies of the revolution anywhere in the world." Within three months, ten Libyans living abroad were killed. Qaddafi frequently isolated himself in his desert camp for long periods of time to meditate and simply be alone. He reportedly began to suffer from depression during this period, even enduring a mental breakdown at one point. It has been speculated that he has a severe personality disorder and exhibits bizarre behavior when under great stress, causing faulty judgment.

Other internal tensions included an assassination attempt in October 1993; riots in 1996 to protest Qaddafi's government; and the withdrawal of Libyan troops from Chad after the dispute with the country—which began in 1973—was ended.

Libya's stance against apartheid in South Africa earned Qaddafi the Order of Good Hope, which was presented by President Nelson Mandela in October 1997. Apartheid was a South African political system lasting nearly 50 years that separated citizens by race, and gave greater privilege to those of European origin. In other words, apartheid recognized and rewarded Caucasians. The Order of Good Hope was the highest honor that South Africa awards a foreigner. Qaddafi and Mandela have visited each other's countries a number of times.

There is no explaining Qaddafi's irresponsible, violent behavior over the years, and his people have had to endure crippling economic and trade sanctions because of his actions. The occasional plus, like the Good Hope Award, while admirable, cannot make up for his many negative actions.

CHAPTER

7

Qaddafi's Sponsorship of Terrorism

On December 21, 1988, groups of college students, tourists, and businesspeople—many of whom were headed home to the United States and family Christmas celebrations—settled onto Pan Am Flight 103, which was traveling from Frankfurt, Germany, to London and on to New York City. Not long into the London-to-New York leg of the trip, a bomb exploded aboard the Boeing 747, killing 270 people, including 189 Americans. As debris rained down, 11 people on the ground in Lockerbie, Scotland, were also killed.

After two years of searching, American investigators discovered a computer chip at the crash site, which linked the explosion to two Libyan undercover agents, Abdelbaset Ali Mohmed al-Megrahi and Al Amin Khalifa Fhimah. Fhimah was a former station manager for Libyan Arab Airlines in Malta, an island in the Mediterranean south

Qaddafi's Sponsorship of Terrorism

The nose section of Pan Am Flight 103, *Maid of the Seas*, after a midair explosion ripped apart the plane on December 21, 1988, over Lockerbie, Scotland. All 259 passengers and crew aboard were killed. Eleven people on the ground were also killed. In 2000, two Libyans accused of the bombing pleaded not guilty. UN diplomats worked with Libya, Britain, and the United States on an agreement whereby the Libyan government would accept responsibility for the bombing, compensate the victims' families, and renounce terrorism. After many years, the Libyan government agreed, and UN sanctions against the country were lifted.

of Italy. The bomb, which had been hidden in a suitcase, was traced to an Air Malta connecting flight.

Megrahi and Fhimah were indicted by the United States and Great Britain on November 14, 1991, and charged with murder, conspiracy to commit murder, and violations of international aviation safety laws. Qaddafi, however, refused to turn over the two men, who had been living in Libya since the bombing, claiming that they would not get a fair trial. Qaddafi taunted the world by saying, "The evidence against Libya is less than a laughable piece of fingernail," according to Ted Gottfried in his book, *Libya: Desert Land in Conflict.*

Despite increasing pressure from other nations and from some critics inside Libya, Qaddafi continued to refuse to extradite the two men. They had been members of the Secret Service, which supported Qaddafi so strongly that it promised that if the men were extradited, it would no longer back Qaddafi's regime. The Secret Service suggested it was highly likely the two men would implicate Qaddafi in the bombing, since it was doubtful that the attack could have occurred without his knowledge and approval. Also, it was probable that the agents would divulge secrets of Libya's involvement with international terrorism. The threat to Qaddafi was obvious.

Frustrated at Qaddafi's lack of cooperation, in 1992 the United Nations Security Council imposed sanctions on Libya, including a ban against international flights into or out of the country, as well as a limitation on the sale of equipment to Libya to be used in the oil industry.

The New York Times of June 24, 1992, quoted a European ambassador as saying, "If Qaddafi fulfills the conditions for lifting United Nations sanctions, he can combat the growing discontent among the populace. But if he extradites the two suspects, the security apparatus, the very pillar of his rule, will turn on him."

EARLY TIES TO TERRORISM

Qaddafi's association with terrorist groups had its beginning shortly after he took control of Libya.

On September 5, 1972, the world was shocked when the peaceful camaraderie of the Olympics was shattered. In the early morning hours, a group of masked terrorists from the Black September Group breached security and attacked the Israeli quarters in the Olympic Village in Munich, Germany, and

Qaddafi's Sponsorship of Terrorism

Osrat Iosef is the daughter of slain Olympic athlete Romano Iosef. Iosef holds a picture of the 11 Israelis killed after their abduction by Palestinian terrorists during the Olympic Games in Munich on September 5, 1972. At the time this photo was taken, August 2002, Iosef was attending a commemoration in Munich for the victims.

kidnapped eleven Israeli athletes. Two hostages were immediately killed, and the remaining nine were massacred several days later, after negotiations failed. Qaddafi openly supported the Black September terrorists, who were a splinter group of the PLO. Five terrorists were killed trying to escape; three were captured; and three escaped to Libya. It was later determined that the weapons used had been smuggled through the Libyan Embassy in West Germany less than two weeks earlier.

Qaddafi called the dead killers "martyr heroes." He buried them with full military honors after a day of Muslim prayers and other ceremonies. Then he granted sanctuary to the three who had returned to Libya and would not allow extradition to West Germany. The West German government traded the three captured terrorists for the crew of a West German plane hijacked by other members of Black September in October 1972. Qaddafi offered the freed terrorists a heroes' welcome, saying, "The cause of the Palestinians is righteous."

Israel labeled Qaddafi an enemy for his role in the killings and retaliated on February 21, 1973, by shooting down a Libyan passenger plane that violated its airspace. All 108 passengers and crew members were killed. Even though it had a nearby airbase with fighter jets ready for flight, Egypt failed to respond to the Libyan airliner's distress call. Qaddafi would have forgiven Anwar Sadat if he had agreed to join Libya in a retaliatory attack. When Sadat refused, Qaddafi called him and his people "cowardly Egyptians."

Later that year, on August 5, 1973, Qaddafi-sponsored terrorists struck again, spraying the Athens airport with machine gun fire. Three passengers waiting to board a flight to New York were killed and thirty-five were wounded. That December 17, thirty-one people were killed when a bomb exploded in the Rome airport. One of the men responsible for the bombing was caught, and he revealed that Qaddafi had ordered the attack in lieu of assassinating U.S. Secretary of State Henry Kissinger. According to this source, Qaddafi was hoping these attacks would separate Israel from its allies and their support.

It seemed to the confused world that there was no rhyme or reason to what groups Qaddafi backed and what causes he financed. Sometimes the groups were not even Muslim or related to the Israeli-Palestinian conflict. For example, he is said to have paid Carlos the Jackal to kidnap oil ministers from Saudi Arabia and Iran. Carlos the Jackal was a notorious Venezuelan terrorist who was believed to have been involved in the Olympic killings. In the late 1970s, he found refuge in Libya and other Arab countries despite an international manhunt. Qaddafi was implicated, too, in activities in other non-Arab countries, including the Irish Republican Army and its ongoing warfare over Northern Ireland. Qaddafi also tried to cause trouble in the United States by preying on independent dissident groups. For example, during the 1970s, he donated more than $300,000 to the Black Panthers, a group of American blacks who used violence to attain their goal of establishing a separate black nation.

Over the years, Qaddafi tried many times, always unsuccessfully, to merge neighboring Arab nations into one unified Arab state, including Egypt, Sudan, Tunisia, Algeria, Syria, and Morocco. Although the leaders of these Arab states pretended to agree with these plans, they had no desire to hand over their power. In the beginning, Qaddafi felt close to Egypt because of shared ideologies and opposition to Israel. But that changed as Sadat made overtures of friendship toward Israel, after realizing that Egypt's anti-Israeli stance alienated it from America and depressed its economy. Sadat visited Israel in 1977, becoming the first Arab leader to do so, and he finally signed the Camp David peace accords in September 1978. The agreement was brokered by President Jimmy Carter and signed by Egypt and Israel after twelve days of talks, resulting in two resolutions. The first was specific to Egypt and Israel and allowed for peace between them. The second concerned the settlement of the Middle East conflict for all countries in the region willing to negotiate with Israel. Qaddafi saw these developments as a betrayal and came to believe that Egypt was an enemy of Libya, and Sadat was "the devil."

On October 6, 1981, Sadat was assassinated by a group of his countrymen. Sadat had recently taken part in the Paris Conference, where he openly declared his anti-Libyan sentiments and reiterated his belief that the United States would not be able to stand firm against Qaddafi. It is widely believed that he was killed, at least in part, for those beliefs, and many believed the assassins were backed by Qaddafi.

In 1979, Russia invaded Afghanistan and forces of the Iranian religious leader, Ayatollah Khomeini, invaded the U.S. Embassy in Tehran, taking American hostages. That December, Qaddafi's police did nothing while Libyan protesters burned the American Embassy in Tripoli. Soon after, Libyan officials were expelled from the United States, and the American Embassy in Tripoli was closed.

ATTACKS INTENSIFY

In the 1980s, incidences of violence connected to Qaddafi and the terrorists he sponsored continued to escalate: A car bomb exploded in April 1983, next to the U.S. Marine barracks at the airport in Beirut, Lebanon. More than 200 Marines and soldiers were killed in the blast, caused by more than six tons of dynamite. In September 1984, sixteen people were killed, including two Americans, when a bomb exploded at the U.S. Embassy annex in Beirut. That December, two Americans were killed and other passengers were tortured when a Kuwaiti airliner was hijacked.

In June 1985, an American pilot was killed and passengers were held hostage on an American plane. In late 1985, an Italian cruise ship was hijacked and an elderly American man was killed in response to a CIA plan to aid opposition groups in attacking Libya. An Egyptian plane was seized in November 1985, and three Israelis and two Americans were killed. At the end of December that year, a radical Palestinian organization led by Abu Nidal, who often based his group in Tripoli, opened fire and threw grenades in the Leonardo da Vinci Airport in

Rome, killing sixteen. Among the dead were five Americans, including an 11-year-old girl. Almost at the same time, members of the same extremist group attacked the airport in Vienna, Austria, killing four people.

Libyan connections were made in all of these acts. Qaddafi's reaction was derision toward the Western world, and blatant support of the terror. It was almost as if he were daring the world to take action against him. Around this time, the British journalist Claire Sterling labeled Qaddafi "the Daddy Warbucks of world terrorism" after the rich father figure in the cartoon, *Little Orphan Annie*.

In 1984, during an anti-Qaddafi demonstration outside the Libyan Embassy in London, a British policewoman was fatally shot. It was believed that someone inside the embassy was responsible, but the Libyan diplomats claimed diplomatic immunity and were never charged. The shooting led to the end of diplomatic relations between Britain and Libya.

On the sixteenth anniversary of his coup, Qaddafi made a speech that in part identified his vision of pan-Arab unity. He said, "This is our homeland from the Atlantic Ocean to the Persian Gulf. This is our single people. We do not recognize the borders which have been drawn up by the colonial powers to partition the single Arab people. We support, as of now, the realization of Arab unity by force. Any Arab side which is capable of realizing Arab unity by force—we support it, accept it, and place our resources at its disposal." When the leaders of many Arab countries rejected his premise, he advocated revolution and added, "We must incite it [revolution] day and night."

For three months at the beginning of 1986, the United States engaged Libyan patrol boats over access to the Gulf of Sidra, an important access point. Since 1973, Libya had claimed that its territorial waters included the entire gulf—a claim the United States disputed. President Ronald Reagan had moved the U.S. Sixth Fleet into the gulf after Qaddafi called it the "Zone of Death" and threatened attack on any U.S. military or

In this 2001 photo, reporters work under a monument of a fist clenching a U.S. warplane built outside Libyan leader Muammar Qaddafi's residence in Tripoli. In 1986, U.S. President Ronald Reagan ordered American warplanes to bomb Tripoli in retaliation for the allegedly Libyan-led fatal terrorist attack on a Berlin discotheque frequented by American troops. One of Qaddafi's daughters was killed during the U.S. air strikes.

commercial ships that entered the zone. During this time, several Libyan Air Force jets were shot down.

In retaliation for the U.S. attack on their Air Force jets, Libyan operatives bombed La Belle discotheque in West Berlin, a bar that was frequented by U.S. military men and women. Three people were killed and more than 200 were injured, many of them American military personnel. Messages from East Berlin to Libyan intelligence agencies were intercepted in early April 1986, and used as evidence to back up President Reagan's decision to bomb specific sites in Libya about two weeks later.

During the height of his involvement with worldwide terrorism, in the 1970s and 1980s, Qaddafi provided twenty training camps for terrorist groups, and six months of basic training and special training in sabotage. Seven thousand terrorists received training in Libya, taught by experts from East Germany and Cuba and reportedly, some former CIA agents. According to a 1985 report, in the previous decade, Libya was involved in 200 terrorist operations worldwide. These incidents injured more than 500 people and killed more than 100, at a cost to Qaddafi of $100 million a year. He did not call these trained murderers terrorists, however, but preferred the term "resistance leaders" or "freedom fighters." He said, "We are the mecca of freedom fighters and their natural ally. We are the first to welcome them, from Ireland to the Philippines."

A commentator on international affairs, the author Walter Laqueur, said of Qaddafi's regime: "Qaddafi's feeling of mission, his lack of restraint and his megalomania gave Libya a notoriety it never would have had otherwise." And Edward Wakin, author of *Contemporary Political Leaders of the Middle East*, wrote, "Qaddafi emerges as a revolutionary who was romantic rather than realistic, a leader who missed an historic opportunity to transform his country; a failed and dangerous dreamer for whom oil and his people paid the bill."

… CHAPTER 8

Fallout from Terrorist Activities: Sanctions and Military Actions

Perhaps the most egregious act of terrorism perpetrated with the knowledge and support of Muammar Qaddafi was the bombing of Pan Am Flight 103. Despite worldwide condemnation and calls for extradition of the two men implicated in the bombing, Qaddafi vehemently denied that Libya had any connection to the explosion and refused to turn over the men to the United States or Great Britain for questioning. On November 14, 1991, those two countries indicted Abdelbaset Ali Mohmed al-Megrahi and Al Amin Khalifa Fhimah on several charges. Qaddafi continued to deny extradition.

Qaddafi's refusal to cooperate with the investigation led the United Nations to impose trade and economic sanctions against Libya. Three resolutions were ultimately passed by the UN Security Council

Fallout from Terrorist Activities: Sanctions and Military Actions

demanding the extradition of the suspects and the end of state-sponsored terrorism by Libya.

In January 1992, Resolution 731 "demanded that Libya accept responsibility for the bombing, disclose all evidence related to it, and pay appropriate compensation to the families of the victims."

Resolution 748 was adopted in April 1992 imposing "an arms and civil aviation embargo on Libya, demanding the closure of all Libyan Arab Airlines offices, and requiring that all states reduce Tripoli's diplomatic appearance abroad." When Libya ignored the two resolutions, the Security Council passed Resolution 883 in November 1993 "tightening the existing sanctions, imposing a limited-assets freeze, and placing an oil technology embargo on Libya."

Ibrahim M. al-Bishari, the Libyan foreign minister, promised the United Nations that his country's 631-member parliament would "take an appropriate stand regarding the matter as soon as possible." But instead, the parliament merely agreed with the official government position. In one of its meetings, when a member complained that the sanctions had caused severe problems for her constituents, Bishari told her that "there are no deprived areas in the great people's republic." This statement was, of course, a lie, as the sanctions were taking their toll.

Despite its belief that Qaddafi had knowledge of the attack, if not actually ordering it, the U.S. government had to proceed cautiously to ensure the safety of Americans and others friendly to the United States within Libya and neighboring countries. The United States also had to be careful not to push the average Libyan into stronger support for Qaddafi through stringent punishments. " . . . Officials at the White House were concerned that the U.S. not push Qaddafi into a corner where he felt there was no other option except to escalate. . . . He had to believe that the benefits of Libyan escalation were not as important to him as the costs of further retaliation from the United States," wrote Raymond Tanter.

Although Qaddafi somewhat conformed to the resolutions, reducing his overt support of international terrorism, he maintained his support of radical Palestinian groups, extremist Islamic groups, and anyone opposed to the Middle East peace process.

The serious hardships caused by the UN sanctions against the import of medical supplies and replacement parts for oil-production and farm equipment not only affected the Libyan people and their economy, but they also damaged the military establishment. All military and technical advisers, including nearly 2,000 from the Soviet Union who had advised the Libyan air defense system, were forced to leave the country. Even so, Qaddafi continued to refuse extradition.

The United Nations refused Qaddafi's offer to try the two bombing suspects in Libyan courts and stood behind the U.S. demands for extradition. The sanctions remained in place, and caused general discontent among Libyans. In late June 1992, a young Libyan in Tripoli was quoted in *The New York Times* as saying that "the best thing that could happen is that the United States bombed again, only this time, managed to get him."

The sanctions did have a far-reaching effect within the country. Electric and telephone service was interrupted, mail delivery was sporadic, and sewer and water systems failed. Food and clothing supplies were skimpy and market shelves were often empty. Medical and hospital equipment was scarce, and school supplies also were in short supply. The people were growing resentful, and the country's only daily newspaper, *Al Fajr al Jadid*, printed an editorial on June 10, 1992, that accused the government of "following a mirage." It went on to say that " . . . we will not follow the mirage with you this time."

On August 5, 1996, the Sanctions Act against Libya and Iran was signed into law with some family members of victims of the Pan Am bombing in attendance. The act, passed unanimously in the House and Senate, represented the overwhelmingly negative feelings that Americans held toward these two nations. Trade with Libya and Iran was made illegal,

Fallout from Terrorist Activities: Sanctions and Military Actions   83

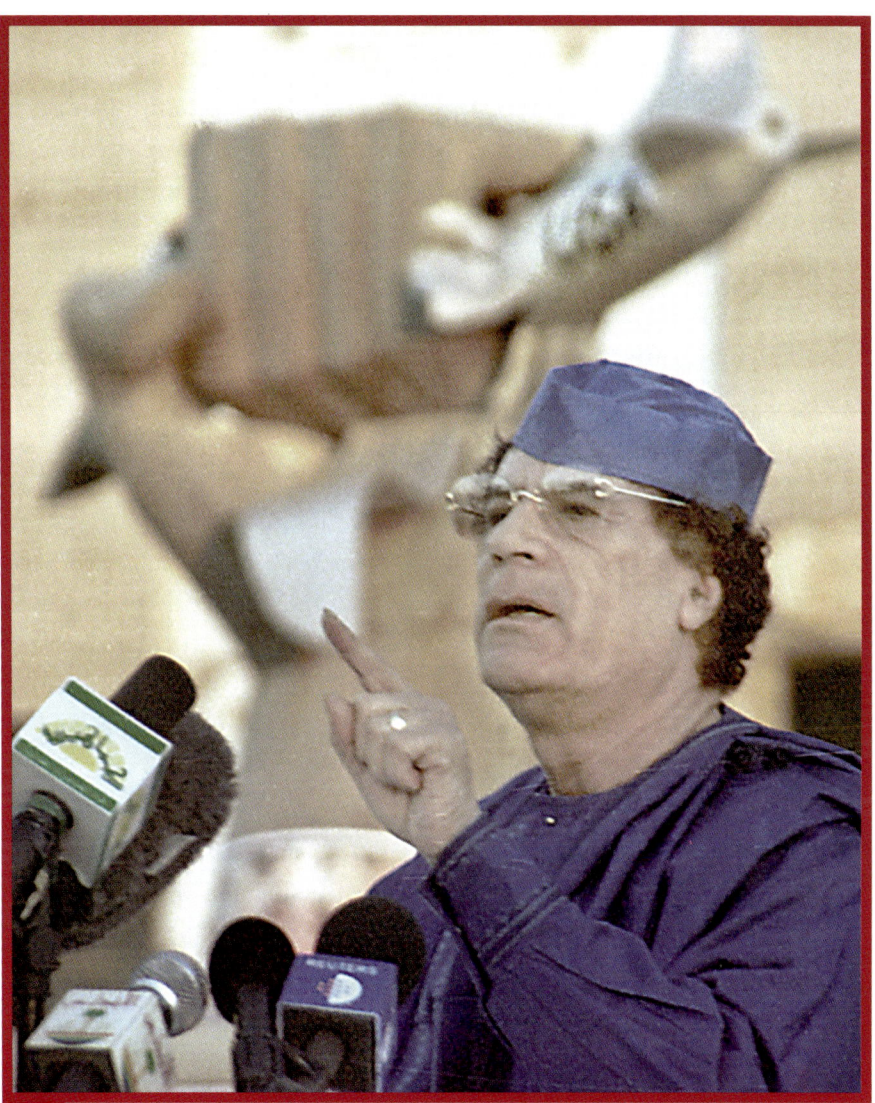

Muammar Qaddafi, during a press conference, February 5, 2001, in Tripoli, Libya. There, 23 years after the terrorist bombing of Pan Am Flight 103 over Lockerbie, Scotland, Libya and France agreed on a deal to compensate the families of the victims. In recent years, in order to remove sanctions against his country, Qaddafi renounced his country's support of terrorism and worked to improve relations with Western Europe and the United States.

and American businesses and those of our allies could be penalized for dealing with them.

"American public opinion was clear: Contain Qaddafi so that he couldn't engage in subversion, terrorism, or chemical weapons proliferation. Qaddafi and Libya became geopolitical outlaws," Tanter wrote.

By the end of the 1990s, Libya claimed that the UN sanctions, along with those instituted by the United States in the 1980s, had cost it more than $19 billion in trade and the loss of more than 20,000 lives because of the inability to obtain foreign medical aid. These figures may be exaggerated, and according to Tanter, for the most part, the sanctions had been more of an "inconvenience than a serious hindrance."

After seven years of the UN sanctions, and the intercession of President Nelson Mandela of South Africa and UN Secretary General Kofi Annan in 1999, Libya finally turned over the suspects. The agreement that Qaddafi negotiated with Annan and Mandela provided that the trial of the two men would be held in the Netherlands under Scottish law, and that the UN sanctions would be lifted. The trial began on May 3, 2000, with a verdict finally reached on January 31, 2001. Megrahi was found guilty and sentenced to life in prison; Fhimah was found not guilty and returned to Libya the following day. On September 12, 2003, the United Nations lifted the sanctions against Libya.

EARLIER AMERICAN SANCTIONS

When the United Nations curtailed trade with and air travel in and out of Libya, it was the second time in a decade that the country had faced imposition of sanctions for its misbehavior. The Americans had put similar restrictions in place in the 1980s.

In early 1981, the U.S. Navy's Sixth Fleet began training exercises in the air and the Gulf of Sidra, which Libya claimed as its territorial waters. In all probability, the training exercises

Fallout from Terrorist Activities: Sanctions and Military Actions 85

Families of the victims of the 1988 terrorist bombing of a Pan Am Airlines flight over Lockerbie, Scotland, listen as the United Nations Security Council discusses an upcoming vote on whether to lift sanctions against Libya. Libya is accused of backing the terrorists involved in the bombing.

were held to send a message to Qaddafi, as the U.S. command knew that the presence of a military force in the region would be beneficial.

Two Libyan planes threatened U.S. Naval aircraft on August 19, 1981, while they were performing routine training procedures, and the two U.S. F-14 fighters shot down the Libyan planes. The Libyan pilots had prepared to attack and had activated the target acquisition radar and guidance systems of their air-to-air missiles, making the U.S. pilots' response justifiable. Nevertheless, Qaddafi called on other Arab leaders to denounce the U.S. downing of the planes. He received no support whatsoever from other Arab leaders, but did gain support at home.

The United States's sanctions on Libya were multilayered. In the hope of ending the country's subversive behavior, its support for terrorism, and its procurement of weapons of mass destruction, especially chemical weapons, the United States banned the import of Libyan oil, froze nearly $1 billion in Libyan assets, and banned U.S. oil companies from operating there. The United States also demanded that all American citizens—about 700 lived there then—return home, ceased the issue of U.S. visas for Libyan nationals, and banned U.S. travel to Libya and the export of American products to that country.

At the time, these economic sanctions may not have had their desired effect, because Libya could buy similar products from other sources and could export its oil to other customers. Qaddafi had been successful in establishing trade relations with European countries and attracting financial investment. Most important, these relationships included oil companies that had invested millions for oil and gas exploration, production, and development agreements. By the mid-1990s, Libya controlled more than 300,000 barrels per day and owned more than 3,000 service stations. Libya also owned several refineries in Europe.

The goal of the United States in imposing sanctions against Libya was to isolate it from the world and punish Qaddafi into submission. Qaddafi's behavior was abhorrent to Americans, and the public tended to support the government in its imposition of sanctions. Limiting trade and other relations, it was felt, would bring Libya "to its senses," creating a sense of cooperation and civility.

Great Britain and other European countries tended to disagree with America's need for punishment and were unable to grasp how a negative action would produce a positive reaction. The American business community tended to agree, however, with the Europeans that the sanctions hurt the "little guy" and that they rarely damaged the lives of those responsible for their imposition.

Fallout from Terrorist Activities: Sanctions and Military Actions

Tanter wrote: "Americans qualify capitalism: They don't want to deal with evil men and women—those who traffic in human suffering. The Founding Fathers created the United States on a principle that all are created equal and deserve a life free from tyranny, which allows for the pursuit of personal endeavors."

MILITARY ACTION

In the mid-1980s, after three years of steady terrorist attacks either sanctioned by Qaddafi or directly ordered by him, President Ronald Reagan had seen enough. On April 15, 1986, the United States attacked Libya, bombing the important port cities of Benghazi and Tripoli, the Tripoli Naval Base, the Benghazi Military Barracks, and the airports within each city. The Bab Al-Aziziya military compound outside Tripoli, which provided a home for Qaddafi and his family, was also a prime target.

When he ordered the attack, Reagan called on people to remember the outrageous actions of the last several years and Qaddafi's flaunting of international law and his complete disregard for human life.

In the early morning of April 15, eighteen F-111 bombers from the U.S. 48th Tactical Fighter Wing took off from Lakenheath, England. While they flew south toward Libya's coast, the U.S. Sixth Fleet was positioned in the Mediterranean with dozens of F-16 jets. Under the control of Vice Admiral Frank Kelso, the fleet commander, were two aircraft carriers, the *Coral Sea* and the *America*; cruisers and destroyers; nuclear-powered submarines; a helicopter carrier; eleven squadrons of attack aircraft protected by four Hawkeye radar planes; and about 1,800 Marines.

All this manpower and firepower sounds impressive and may sound like more than was needed. But Libya had been building up its military for years and was well armed, thanks to Soviet suppliers and support. "Libya had more tanks per head of population than any other country," wrote David Blundy

The harbor of Tripoli. Since economic sanctions against Libya were lifted in 2003, Arab and European counterparts, together with Libyan experts, seek to stimulate tourism in this beautiful Mediterranean city.

and Andrew Lycett in their book, *Qaddafi and the Libyan Revolution*. Blundy was a reporter based in Tripoli during the bombing raid. Although the country was well stocked with firepower and equipment, its army was not well trained and was fairly unreliable. After the attack, Libya found itself pretty much on its own. The Soviets, who had provided hundreds of advisers and offered its help, urged restraint. Soviet warships were anchored in a far corner of the Mediterranean Sea, but did not race to the rescue; instead, the fleet landed in Tripoli's port two weeks after the attack.

In spite of the U.S. plan to strike only targets that could be precisely defined and had been shown to be related to terrorist and military activity, apartments and villas on the outskirts of

Fallout from Terrorist Activities: Sanctions and Military Actions

the city were demolished, the French Embassy was damaged, and a park and playground were destroyed. Shortly after the attack, journalists were paraded around the damaged civilian areas in an attempt to elicit the world's sympathy.

Reagan believed areas of Tripoli and Benghazi were terrorism centers—training camps and shelters—and used this as additional justification for the attack, which killed dozens of civilians, including Qaddafi's 15-month-old adopted daughter, Hanna. Two of his sons, Saif-al-Arab, 4, and Hamis, 3, were injured. Qaddafi's home and office were in a bunker within the Bab Al-Aziziya compound, which was built like a fortress and protected by soldiers, tanks, and other equipment. The compound was also the center of Qaddafi's communications setup, through which he stayed in close touch with his officers. Blundy and Lycett wrote that Qaddafi's wife and children lived in a plush apartment near the Bedouin tent that Qaddafi called home. He called Qaddafi's home an "odd combination of Bedouin tradition and high tech" with a television and stereo equipment. Tennis courts provided outdoor entertainment.

The attack on Qaddafi's compound at Aziziya was a failure. The administration building remained unscathed, and Qaddafi, who had been underground during the attack, remained unharmed.

Some thought a U.S.-sponsored coup was under way. For several days after the attack, intermittent shooting and fighting disrupted the city and there were reports of revolts in several military groups. Even though Libya denied that any military targets had been destroyed, a warehouse in Benghazi was hit. Soldiers and a military helicopter were found inside, and the warehouse was surrounded by barbed wire. Nevertheless, Libyan officials described it at first as a "powdered milk factory." Eventually, they did relent and admitted that the site had been used for "something military."

Because Qaddafi remained in hiding for several days, rumors flew that he had been killed or overthrown. Soon enough, though, he appeared on Libyan television and announced that the country had won a "great victory." He called on the people to "turn on your lights and dance in the streets." He added, "We are not afraid of America!"

But Qaddafi's confident speeches did not match the performance of his expensive military. He had been "caught unprepared with defenses that had failed abysmally," wrote Blundy and Lycett. Also, suicide bombers, who were supposed to hit targets in Europe and America if Libya was attacked, never materialized.

The attack was followed by a political maneuver to "coordinate covert, diplomatic, military, and public actions to destabilize the Qaddafi regime," according to John Poindexter, the U.S. national security adviser at the time. When the Libyan people united briefly behind Qaddafi after the attack, the exiled former Libyan Foreign Minister Mansour Kikhia summed it up this way: "Squeezing the Libyan people so they in turn squeeze Qaddafi out does not work."

Qaddafi and his aide, Major Abdul Salam Jalloud, called Reagan's attack "savage, barbaric aggression" and called Prime Minister Margaret Thatcher of Britain a "child murderer" because of her cooperation with the United States. On the weather map shown on Libyan TV, Britain and the United States were marked out in black. Qaddafi also referred to the Americans and British as "a species which are between pigs and human beings and have not developed yet to become ordinary human beings."

Thatcher, known as "The Iron Lady" for her decisive and self-confident nature, was criticized for her support of the U.S. attack on Libya, but she remained firm in her decision to allow American aircraft to fly out of British air bases. She was sometimes called Reagan's "poodle," a lap dog that did what it was told. She was far from that, however, telling the House of Commons that a "refusal to take action against terrorism would mean that Britain was supine and passive in the face of that terrorism."

Fallout from Terrorist Activities: Sanctions and Military Actions

The United States was criticized at a meeting of the United Nations, and other Arab leaders were full of praise for Qaddafi's "brave stand." He had managed to bring Libya into the spotlight as a small country that had dared to defy the United States and survived.

Even though they were critical of the U.S. operation, European officials meeting late in April in Luxembourg agreed to "limit the size of Libyan foreign missions in Europe and restrict the movements of Qaddafi's diplomats." During the annual economic summit the next month of the G-7 countries, Canada, France, Italy, Japan, the United Kingdom, and West Germany joined the United States in issuing a condemnation of "international terrorism in all its forms, of its accomplices and of those, including governments, who sponsor or support it." The statement prompted Secretary of State George Shultz to say that the message being sent to Qaddafi was, "You've had it, pal!"

Apparently the campaign had some success in curbing Qaddafi's support of terrorist groups. His rhetoric softened, and fewer terrorist plots were uncovered or accomplished with Libyan backing. The U.S. State Department reported that the number of terrorist incidents linked to Libya dropped from nineteen in 1986 to six each in 1987 and 1988. Nevertheless, U.S. intelligence kept a close eye on Qaddafi's top leaders and their communications.

After the attack, Qaddafi began to move his living quarters and office frequently, rarely sleeping in the same place for more than two nights in a row. It was said that the strikes seemed to temporarily cripple his morale and increase opposition against him. Those close to him reported that he was also shaken, confused and uncharacteristically subdued. But ultimately, the attack served to rally the people around Qaddafi, and the symbol of opposition to Western imperialism.

Reagan's objective of curtailing Qaddafi's involvement with terrorist groups came without the commitment of many troops and without a long-term war. Secretary of Defense Caspar Weinberger later wrote in his memoirs: "The purpose of our plan was to teach Qaddafi and others the lesson that the practice of terrorism would not be free of cost to themselves. That indeed, they would pay a terrible price for practicing it."

Weinberger also wrote: "Nothing was heard from Qaddafi for many months after that attack, making this all the vindication that anyone should need of our correctness in rebuilding our military strength and in deciding when to use it." He also called this operation a textbook example of successful intervention, largely because top Pentagon officials had insisted that "we assemble sufficient forces, and act decisively and effectively to achieve all of the president's objectives."

CHAPTER

9

Libya Today and Qaddafi's Legacy

Libya, perched at the uppermost tip of Africa and about three times the size of Texas, is one of the wealthiest Arab nations. Because of the vast oil reserves discovered in the late 1950s, the country went from being one of the poorest during the previous decade, when its leading export was scrap metal scavenged from the tanks and trucks that littered the desert landscape after World War II, to one of the richest.

During the early days of the Cold War, the United States paid Libya $1 million a year to maintain a large Air Force base outside of Tripoli. Planes loaded with long-range nuclear weapons crowded the fields, ready to drop their bombs on the Soviet Union if it was necessary. The original lease agreement for Wheelus Field, signed by U.S. President Dwight D. Eisenhower and King Idris in 1954, called for payments of $4 million through 1960, and $1 million thereafter.

The market in Tripoli. A woman walks hand-in-hand with a little girl past luggage shops in this ancient city, which has been a flourishing Mediterranean port since the eleventh century.

By 1957, Libya's sympathies swayed toward the Soviet Union, with its promise of advisers, weapons, and money, causing the United States to increase its agreement by $2.5 million.

In 1962, when Libyan oil production had risen, Libyans became concerned about how the oil money would be distributed. The CIA reported to President John F. Kennedy that year that "Libya, ruled by an aged and ailing king, rich in oil, and geographically accessible, was a tempting target for Arab radicals" from surrounding countries. Kennedy was advised to encourage the Libyans to pursue "the orderly economic development of the country."

But the king and his inner circle funneled much of the oil money into their own pockets and continued to finance Libya's economic development with the rent money from Wheelus Field. During the mid-1960s, the strategic importance of this air base declined as B-52s were no longer stationed there.

The young Muammar Qaddafi overthrew King Idris with little resistance. The United States was concerned about Qaddafi's philosophical beliefs and approach to governing. According to Douglas Little in *American Orientalism: The United States and the Middle East Since 1945*, implications of the revolution worried U.S. policymakers because "it combined elements of Libyan nationalism, pan-Arab Socialism, and Islamic revivalism." The belief was that Qaddafi would not get involved with the Soviet Union because "Islam seemed incompatible with Communism.

About six weeks after overthrowing King Idris, Qaddafi made the following statement in a speech: "We accept no bases, no foreigner, no colonialist, no intruder, and we will liberate our territory . . . whatever the cost." Both Britain and the United States evacuated their respective air bases in the spring of 1970, hoping to avoid conflict between their countries and Libya. Throughout that year, the United States continued to believe that the religious nature of the takeover would prevent the Soviets from making inroads in Libya. However, tanks and other equipment began to arrive, followed by Qaddafi's revocation of all foreign concessions within the Libyan oil industry. Exactly four years after seizing power, on September 1, 1973, Qaddafi nationalized the industry, controlling oil output, prices, and profits.

The Green Book, Qaddafi's three-volume book, outlined his ideology and plans for a "Muslim cultural revolution" financed by the money earned by the export of oil. Little wrote that Qaddafi's ultimate goal was to "undermine Western influence throughout the Middle East."

He added: "Much of Qaddafi's ideology—his critique of imperialism, his focus on Arab socialism, and his calls for direct democracy—was all too familiar to U.S. policymakers who had been struggling to contain revolutionary nationalism in the Muslim world for two decades. What stood out in *The Green Book*, however, was the Third Universal Theory, which claimed that by returning to the fundamentals of Islam, Libyans could lead Muslims everywhere along a 'Third Way' toward economic development and political change that rejected both capitalism and Communism."

By the late 1970s, Qaddafi had expelled most non-Muslims, supported Islamic wars in Chad and the Philippines, and had given money and other support to terrorists around the world. By the end of that decade, many in the U.S. government regarded Qaddafi as an unpredictable menace. President Jimmy Carter discontinued diplomatic relations between the United States and Libya in 1980 after Libya was added to the list of outlaw states suspected of supporting international terrorism, along with Cuba and North Korea.

Little wrote that in a bit more than ten years, what had begun as a peaceful reform had been transformed into a "violent anti-Western revolution."

Since the mid-1990s, however, Qaddafi's reputation within other Arab and African nations has greatly improved. He is considered moderate and responsible by many in the Arab world. Among African leaders, Qaddafi has been at his post the longest, and because of this, is often considered wise. He has retained his strong stance against Israel, but has become increasingly cooperative with the United States and other Western countries.

Since the turn of the twenty-first century, Qaddafi has reached out to the Western world on several levels. After the attacks on the World Trade Center and the Pentagon on September 11, 2001, he was among the first to denounce Al Qaeda and its actions, saying, "Irrespective of the conflict with America, it is a human duty to show sympathy with the American people and be with them at these horrifying and awesome events which are bound to awaken human conscience."

Libya Today and Qaddafi's Legacy

Libya accepted responsibility for the 1988 Pan Am bombing over Lockerbie, Scotland, and ended up paying $4 million to each of the victims' families in mid-2003. The United Nations lifted its sanctions shortly thereafter.

WHY THE CHANGE?

Theories abound about Qaddafi's seeming about-face. During the 1990s, oil prices dropped sharply, so some think he has had to find other ways to strengthen the country. The continued pressures placed on his people through the UN and U.S. sanctions and the increasing disapproval over his tactics from Western countries and within the Arab world may be another reason. But the most likely reason Qaddafi has seemed to change is that his goals simply did not materialize. The terrorists he supported around the world did not meet their objectives; Arab nations did not band together as one pan-Arab state; and the end of the Cold War and the fall of the Soviet Union made Qaddafi's main target, the United States, even stronger.

With the overthrow of Saddam Hussein's regime in the spring of 2003, Qaddafi voluntarily opened his country to United Nations inspectors in search of the weapons of mass destruction that he admitted he was producing and concealing. Since President George W. Bush invaded Iraq based on claims of existing weapons of mass destruction—nuclear, chemical, and biological—it is possible that Qaddafi was fearful of a similar fate should he not be forthcoming about his weapons. In fact, a Libyan intelligence agent was quoted in the March 8, 2004, issue of *Newyorker.com* as saying that "Qaddafi is very pragmatic and studied the timing. It was the right time. The United States wanted to have a success story, and he banked on that."

Although the diplomatic efforts of the United States and Britain certainly carried weight in Qaddafi's decision to open up to international weapons investigators, it is accepted that the

Libyan leader Muammar Qaddafi salutes his armed forces during a parade in Tripoli, September 7, 1999. The parade marks the revolution's 30th anniversary and the opening of an Organisation of African Unity (OAU) summit.

implied threat of violence against Libya was enough to change Qaddafi's mind. According to an *Insight* magazine article from March 15, 2004, Qaddafi believed he could continue to get away with his "clandestine nuclear weapons program" until September 11, when he realized it would be in his best interests to cooperate proactively after he saw the determined response of the Bush administration.

When troops invaded Iraq on March 19, 2003, Qaddafi ordered talks to begin with the United States and Britain. "The Iraq war made it clear that the U.S. and the U.K. were serious about going after countries with WMD," said a British official in the *Insight* article. He added that Libya continued to work on its weapons of mass destruction program even while talks were under way to turn over weapons and plans. But the interception of a large shipment of centrifuge components, what a U.S. official called "the guts of his [Qaddafi's] program," essentially broke the Libyan nuclear program.

The confiscation of these components encouraged Libya to invite intelligence teams into the country. Then came the event that *Insight* said "sealed the fate of Qaddafi's program." In early December 2003, Qaddafi watched on television as U.S. soldiers pulled Saddam Hussein from a "spider hole" in the ground near Tikrit. The former dictator, normally fastidious to a fault, was gaunt, dirty, and unshaven. As the world—and Qaddafi—watched, Hussein's hair was inspected for lice and his mouth for sores. Qaddafi was "stunned" and "traumatized" by the capture of his contemporary, according to *Insight*. Apparently, the psychological toll was great: Less than two weeks later, Qaddafi announced that he had invited Western officials to inspect his weapons of mass destruction programs and to oversee their dismantling.

According to *Insight*, a Western ambassador in Tripoli "believes that Qaddafi understood that his revolution could not continue unless he delivered more prosperity to Libyans, and the only way to do that was by renewing relations with the West."

In the spring of 2004, Qaddafi addressed a large gathering of more than 600 Libyan political figures. The group also included a seven-member delegation from the U.S. House of Representatives and more than 100 officials from other countries. His long speech can be boiled down to one fact: Yesterday's enemies are today's friends.

Insight magazine printed the following report of the speech: "In a brutally self-critical account of Libya's past support for terrorist movements around the world, Qaddafi concluded that Libya had paid a high price for its adventures, reaping only isolation, international embargoes and underdevelopment. In case after case, he told his countrymen, Libya had helped groups such as the Irish Republican Army, the Palestine Liberation Organization and the African National Congress. Now they had all made their separate peace, leaving Libya behind to continue fighting. 'Are we more Irish than the Irish?' Qaddafi asked. 'Are we more Palestinian than the Palestinians? . . . How can Yasser Arafat enter the White House and we not improve our relations with the United States?' "

Qaddafi continued: "No one separated Libya from the world community. Libya voluntarily separated itself from others. No one has imposed sanctions on us or punished us. We have punished ourselves. . . . The struggles [we have supported] are finished; the battle is finished . . . now people are shaking hands. So should only we stay enemies?"

About Libya's weapons of mass destruction program, Qaddafi said in the speech: "We got rid of it. It was a waste of time. It cost too much money." He called on all countries to get rid of weapons of mass destruction, including the United States, Russia, China, India, and Pakistan. He said, "If there is any aggression against Libya now, the whole world will come to defend Libya. Yesterday, that was not the case." He also asked the United States for help with the technology needed to develop his economy and for the opportunity to join in ventures with United States businesses.

Representative Curt Weldon, a Republican congressman from Pennsylvania, was part of the U.S. delegation. He is quoted in *Insight* as saying, "We were part of history tonight. Col. Qaddafi's statements were unequivocal. There were no ifs, ands, or buts. It reminds me of the sea change that occurred when the Berlin Wall came down, or when Boris Yeltsin stood on top of a tank in front of the Russian White House. As startling as it is to us, we'd better take advantage of it."

As of the summer of 2004, Libya has lived up to its promise to deliver plans and dismantle weapons programs, and abandon its support of terrorism. The United States hoped that other rogue nations, like North Korea, Syria, and Iran, were watching closely and understood that they would be rewarded well if they cooperated and turned over all weapons of mass destruction.

Thousands of tons of chemical weapons have been found in Libya to date, along with a nuclear weapons program. These weapons are being systematically destroyed. Some have been sent to the United States where they are securely locked away, and a chemical plant in Rabta has been converted to manufacture legitimate pharmaceuticals. According to *USnews.com*, Libyan officials were very cooperative with inspectors. If a site was locked or blocked, orders came from above—presumably from Qaddafi himself—to unlock or unblock it. Some of Libya's military personnel opposed Qaddafi's decision to give up the weapons, plans, and equipment, but their anger did not stop Qaddafi.

According to a report issued by the inspectors, most of the materials used to create nuclear weapons had apparently not been assembled. "I'm not impressed by what I've seen," a senior nonproliferation official was quoted in the same *Newyorker.com* article by Seymour M. Hersh. "It was not a well-developed program—not a serious research-and-development approach to make use of what they bought. It was useless. But I was struck by what the Libyans were able to buy. What's on the market is absolutely horrendous." As shown by these revelations, it is possible to buy the materials needed to create these deadly weapons, even if the program to put them to use is not fully established. Additionally, inspectors found blueprints for building car-sized nuclear bombs, a discouraging discovery.

Prime Minister Tony Blair of Britain visited Qaddafi in Tripoli in the spring of 2004, praising him and welcoming him as an ally in the war on terrorism.

As sincere as Qaddafi may be about rebuilding his country and rejoining the international community as a respected member, he will need Western help and probably knows that. Despite the healthy appearance of the market in Tripoli, downtown streets are unpaved, phone service is unreliable, and foreigners are often mistrusted. Libya's universities are graduating record numbers of students who cannot find work. Either the country will lose its best and brightest as they immigrate to other countries where they can be productive, or a new revolution will take place.

Qaddafi's son, Seif al-Islam el-Qaddafi, 31, has become increasingly involved in Libya's politics since 1999, advocating for modernization and a new openness to the West. Seif is the head of the Qaddafi Foundation for Charitable Organizations and is thought to have been behind getting his father to take responsibility for the bombing of Flight 103. The foundation has also advocated for political prisoners and against torture. Amnesty International was invited to Libya for the first time in fifteen years because of Seif's beliefs in human rights. The group found continued human rights abuses, but said in its report: "We are pleased with the unprecedented access we were given by the Libyan authorities and others, particularly to prisoners. We look forward to a serious engagement by Libya with a process of accountability for past violations and reform for the future." In April 2004, Qaddafi ended the practice of arrests without warrants and ratified international anti-torture conventions.

Libyan leader Muammar Qaddafi (center) and his sons Al-Saadi (left), president of Libya's soccer federation and a national team player, and, Seif al-Islam (right), chair of the Qaddafi Foundation for Charitable Organizations. Libyans suspect that power will eventually pass from Muammar Qaddafi to one of his sons, who increasingly share the spotlight with Qaddafi.

The travel ban and most sanctions, which strangled Libya and damaged its economy for so long, have been lifted. Full diplomatic relations are in the process of being restored, something unimaginable only a few years ago. Libyan businessmen court American engineers and their technology in hopes of reviving the sagging oil industry as well as American food and pharmaceutical companies to create a mutually beneficial relationship. And travel agents and others are eager to open the country to Western tourists and their money. Successful economic development will be the cornerstone of the new Libya, they believe.

Reform is happening in Libya, but a hallmark of an open society, free speech, is slow to come, as citizens continue to fear recrimination for speaking their mind. The *Insight* magazine reporter, accompanied by a U.S. congressman, approached ordinary people in the market, and found they were "reluctant to discuss politics . . . but all expressed delight at the prospect of renewed U.S.–Libyan ties." A Libyan electrical engineer is quoted as saying, "If you want to improve the human-rights situation, the best thing you can do is to open a U.S. Embassy in Tripoli and to be here with your press. If anything happens, you will see it soon enough." Another Libyan, a spokesman for the National Front for the Salvation of Libya, agrees that change will come if the United States maintains pressure on human rights issues in the country. "Qaddafi feels his regime is threatened if he does not cooperate with the United States. That's why he has made concessions. The United States should press him on human-rights violations, and ultimately press for a new constitution and a new system of legal government."

Today, satellite dishes beam Western television shows into Libyan living rooms. Cell phones keep people connected, and Internet access is cheap.

Those who dare to speak out against the regime are quoted as saying they are "sick of Qaddafi's family"—wondering aloud, "Who appointed them to rule our country?" Graffiti saying "Today, Saddam. Tomorrow, Qaddafi" appeared on walls in Tripoli after Saddam's capture, and an editor at a government newspaper was fired after opining that Qaddafi should become Libya's president, giving up the role of dictator. Open dissent is healthy for a developing democracy, and in fact, is another hallmark of a free society.

It is difficult to predict how future generations will view Qaddafi. Was he a man of vision and fierce national and religious pride; the savior of his country and leader of the masses, who reinstated a belief in the Islamic religion? Or will he be remembered most for his overt support of terrorism? Still known to his countrymen as "the leader of the Revolution" or simply "The Leader," he holds nearly total power even after 35 years at the helm. At 62, he is young enough to hold on to that power for a while to come. Even as Libya opens up to Western development in business and investment, it remains a dictatorship. *USnews.com* said that the Libyan elite envision a Chinese-style evolution: "Open up the economy, but hold on tight to political power." The director of the Libyan Jihad Center for Historical Studies, Mohammed Jerary, who was educated at the University of Wisconsin, is quoted as saying, "We want democracy—but with your assistance, not your force."

CHRONOLOGY

1942   Qaddafi was born in Sirte.

1951   **December 24**   Libya gains independence; King Idris I is appointed.

1956   Qaddafi organizes the first of his revolutionary cells in high school.

1963   Qaddafi graduates from the University of Libya with a law degree.

1964   Qaddafi graduates from the Benghazi Military Academy at the top of his class. He is commissioned a lieutenant in the Army.

1969   **September 1**   Qaddafi stages a successful "bloodless" coup, overthrowing King Idris I. He proclaims the country a Socialist Libyan Arab Republic.

1970   Qaddafi leads a campaign to "Libyanize" the country by erasing all foreign influences.

1971   Libya joins Egypt and Syria in forming the Federation of Arab Republics, which lasts only two years because of friction between Egypt and Libya.

1975   Qaddafi publishes the first volume of the three-volume *The Green Book* on his philosophy of government.

1981   United States shoots down two Libyan Air Force jets.

1986   Sanctions are imposed by the United States for terrorist activities.

1986   **March 24**   U.S. Navy ships confront Libyan forces, sinking two Libyan patrol boats.

1986   **April 5**   Libya is implicated in a deadly bombing at a West German disco.

1986   **April 15**   United States bombs Libya.

1988   **December 21**   Pan Am Flight 103 is bombed, killing 270; two Libyans are later indicted in connection with the attack.

1993   **November 11**   UN Security Council tightens sanctions as Libya continues to refuse to extradite the Flight 103 bombing suspects.

2003   Libya accepts responsibility for the Pan Am bombing and agrees to pay restitution to the victims' families. Libya begins to open its borders to UN weapons inspectors; weapons of mass destruction and nuclear plans are confiscated and destroyed.

2004   Sanctions are eased and dropped; diplomatic relations are tentatively reinstituted.

FURTHER READING

Bearman, Jonathan. *Qaddafi's Libya.* London and New Jersey: Zed Books, Ltd., 1986.

Blundy, David & Lycett, Andrew. *Qaddafi and the Libyan Revolution.* New York, NY: Little, Brown & Company, 1987.

Cooley, John K. *Libyan Sandstorm.* New York: Holt, Rinehart and Winston, 1982.

Gottfried, Ted. *Libya: Desert Land in Conflict.* Brookfield, CT: The Millbrook Press, 1994.

Haley, P. Edward. *Qaddafi and the United States Since 1969.* New York: Praeger Publishers, 1984.

Hersh, Seymour M. The Deal. *The Newyorker.com.* March 8, 2004.

Laqueur, Walter. *The Age of Terrorism.* Boston: Little, Brown and Company, 1987.

Little, Douglas. *American Orientalism: The United States and the Middle East Since 1945.* Chapel Hill, NC: The University of North Carolina Press, 2002.

Sicker, Martin. *The Making of A Pariah State.* New York: Praeger Publishers, 1987.

Tames, Richard. *Take a Trip to Libya.* New York, NY: Franklin Watts, 1989.

Tanter, Raymond. *Rogue Regimes: Terrorism and Proliferation.* New York, NY: St. Martin's Press, 1998.

Timmerman, Kenneth R. *How George W. Bush Got Qaddafi's Attention.* Insight Magazine, March 15, 2004.

Wakin, Edward. *Contemporary Political Leaders of the Middle East.* New York, NY: Facts on File, Inc, 1996.

Willis, Terri. *Libya: Enchantment of the World.* New York, NY: Children's Press; Grolier Publishing, 1999.

Libya . . . in Pictures: Visual Geography Series. Minneapolis, MN: Lerner Publications, 1996.

INDEX

Adassa, 20
Afghanistan, Soviet invasion of, 76
African National Congress, 16, 100
agriculture, 28
    and Qaddafi, 55, 56
    and sanctions, 82
    and water, 58–60
Aisha (mother), 34
Al Fajr al Jadid, 82
Al Qaeda, 96
Algeria, and Qaddafi desiring one unified Arab state, 75
Al-Kufrah, 29
Allah, 26
America (aircraft carrier), 87
Amnesty International, 102
ancestor worship, 25
animals, in Libya, 30
animism, 25
Annan, Kofi, 84
apartheid, Qaddafi against, 69
aquifers, 58
Arabic language, 22, 28
Arabs, 22
    Egyptian, 22
    Libyans as, 28
    and Nasser, 36–37
    and opposition to Qaddafi, 16, 62, 63, 65–66, 74, 75–76, 85
    and Qaddafi desiring one unified state, 14, 16, 23, 36, 41, 44, 61, 75, 77
    and support of Qaddafi, 96
    and United States bombing Libya, 16, 91
army. *See* Libyan Army
Athens, and Qaddafi supporting attack on passengers in airport, 74

Bab Al-Aziziya, United States bombing, 87, 89
Basic People's Congress, 49
Beatte Peak (*Bikku Bitti*), 27, 28
Bedouins, 32, 33, 36
Benghazi, 28, 30
    and Idris I, 23
    United States bombing, 14, 16, 87, 89
Benghazi Military Academy, Qaddafi attending, 39
Berbers, 20, 21, 22, 25, 33, 50
biological weapons, and Paris Conference, 68.
    See also weapons of mass destruction
Bishari, Ibrahim M. al-, 81
Black Panthers, Qaddafi supporting, 75
Black September Group, and Qaddafi supporting attack on Israeli athletes at Olympics, 72–74, 75
Blair, Tony, 102
Blundy, David, 87–88, 89, 90
"Brother Colonel," Qaddafi as, 49

camels, 30
Camp David peace accords, 75
Canada, and United States bombing Libya, 91
capitalism, Qaddafi against, 46
Carlos the Jackal, 75
Carter, Jimmy, 66–67, 75, 96
Carthage, 20
Castro, Fidel, 64
cave paintings, 52
Chad
    Libya in conflict with, 63, 65–66
    Qaddafi supporting Islamic wars in, 96
    withdrawal of Libyan troops from, 69

INDEX

chemical weapons
  and Paris Conference, 68
  Qaddafi agreeing to destruction and confiscation of, 101
  and United States imposing sanctions on Libya, 86.
  See also weapons of mass destruction
Christians, and Qaddafi, 46
CIA
  and aiding opposition groups in Libya, 76
  and Qaddafi, 42, 44
cities, Qaddafi encouraging population shift to, 50
Cold War, 93–94, 97
communication, and Qaddafi, 102, 104
Communism, and Qaddafi, 46, 95. *See also* Soviet Union
constitution
  and Idris I, 25
  and Libya's independence, 23
  and Qaddafi, 46
Coral Sea (aircraft carrier), 87
Cyrenaica, 23, 28–30, 34

Darnah, 28
democracy, 18–19, 104–105
  and Qaddafi, 18–19, 44
desert, 28, 30, 31, 52
  Sahara, 32, 52, 53
direct democracy, Qaddafi on, 44
disarmament, Qaddafi offering voluntary, 13–14

economy, 28, 29–30
  and Idris I, 24, 93–95
  and Qaddafi, 14, 16, 18, 44, 46–47, 48–49, 51, 53–57, 63, 69, 102, 103, 105

and water, 58–60.
  See also oil; sanctions; water
education
  and population shift to cities, 50
  and Qaddafi, 14, 47–48, 54, 55
Egypt
  and Israel, 67, 74, 75–76
  and Libya, 13, 16, 63, 65–67, 75–76
  and Nasser, 36–37, 42, 50, 61, 65
  and Qaddafi desiring one unified Arab state, 75
  and Qaddafi supporting capture of plane, 76
  and Sadat, 65, 66–67, 74, 75–76
  and *Voice of the Arabs* radio program, 36
Egyptian Arabs, 22
Eisenhower, Dwight D., 93
employment, and Qaddafi, 55
ergs, 28
Esso Oil Company, 53
Ethiopia, Soviet Union supporting, 67
Europe
  and United States bombing Libya, 91
  and United States sanctions, 86
European Union, and oil, 65
Exxon, 56, 57

Farouk I, 36
Federation of Arab Republics, 65–66
Fezzan, 23, 28, 37–38
Fhimah, Al Amin Khalifa, 70–72, 80, 84
Five Pillars, 27
food shortages, and Qaddafi, 56

INDEX

France
    and destruction of French airplane, 16
    and Libya's independence, 23, 35
    Qaddafi against, 14
    and United States bombing Libya, 91
    and World War II, 23
Free Officers' Movement, 36, 41

G-7 countries, and United States bombing Libya, 91
Gabriel, Angel, 26
General People's Committee, 49
General People's Congress, 49
General Secretariat, 49
Geneva Protocol, 68
Germany, and World War II, 32
Gottfried, Ted, 22–23, 72
government, Qaddafi's approach to, 14, 36, 42, 44–51, 95–96
Great Britain
    and aid to Libya before oil discovery, 53
    and air base in Libya, 95
    and diplomatic relations with Qaddafi, 102
    and discovery of oil, 53
    and end of diplomatic relations with Libya, 77
    and Idris I, 24
    Libya in talks with giving up weapons of mass destruction, 17, 99
    and Libya's independence, 23, 35
    and military bases in Libya, 24
    Qaddafi against, 14
    and support of Qaddafi's coup, 42
    and United States bombing Libya, 90
    and United States sanctions, 86
    and World War II, 23, 32
Great Man-Made River Project, 58–60
Green Book, The, 14, 45–49, 95–96
Green Mountain (*Al-Jabal al-Akhda*), 28–29

Hammer, Armand, 57
health care
    and population shift to cities, 50
    and Qaddafi, 55
    and sanctions, 82, 84
Hersh, Seymour M., 101
hospitals, and Qaddafi, 54
housing, and Qaddafi, 14, 54, 55
human rights, and Qaddafi, 102, 103–104
hunter-gatherers, early Libyans as, 20
hunting and gathering, 53
Hussein, Saddam, 17, 64, 68, 97, 99

Idris I, 23–25, 55, 93, 94–95
    and oil, 53–54, 56
    Qaddafi overthrowing, 12, 14, 36, 37–39, 41–44, 61, 95
imams, and Israel, 25
infrastructure, and Qaddafi, 18, 51, 53–55
Insight magazine, 99, 101, 103
Iran
    and Khomeini invading American Embassy in Tehran, 76
    and Libya's destruction of weapons of mass destruction, 101

INDEX

and Libya's support in Iran-Iraq war, 67
and Qaddafi paying Carlos the Jackel to kidnap oil ministers, 75
and United States sanctions against, 82, 84
Iran–Iraq war, 67, 68
Iraq
   and Egypt, 36
   and Hussein, 68, 97, 99
   and Iran–Iraq War, 67, 68
   and poison gas, 68
   and United States invasion, 97, 99
Irish Republican Army, 16, 75, 100
irrigation systems, and Qaddafi, 55
Islam, 22
   beliefs of, 26, 27
   on education for women, 47
   introduction of, 25
   and Libyan constitution, 46
   as main religion, 25
   and Muhammad, 25–26
   and Nasser, 36
   and Qaddafi, 12–13, 14, 34, 39, 44, 44–45, 46, 47–48, 49–50, 51, 95, 96
   and Sanusi, 26, 34
   Shiite, 25
   spread of, 26
   Sunni, 25, 34, 44–45
"Islamic Socialism," Qaddafi's new government as, 44–45, 46
Israel, 67
   and Egypt, 63, 74, 75–76
   and Nasser, 36–37
   and Qaddafi, 13, 14, 37–38, 72–74, 75–76, 82, 96

and Qaddafi against peace with Palestine, 63–64, 67
and Qaddafi supporting Black September Group's attack on athletes at Olympics, 72–74, 75
and shooting down Libyan passenger plane, 74
Sunni Muslims against, 25
and United States, 57
Italy
   and history, 34–35
   and Libya as colony, 34–35
   and Libya gaining independence, 23, 37
   Qaddafi against, 14
   and United States bombing Libya, 91
   and World War II, 32.
   See also Rome

Jafara Plain, 28
Jalloud, Abdul Salam, 90
Jamahiriya, 14, 18
Japan, and United States bombing Libya, 91
Jebel Nefusah, 28
Jebel Zelten, 53
Jerary, Mohammed, 105
Jews, 25
   and Qaddafi, 46.
   See also Israel
jihad, and Israel, 25
Jordan, and Egypt, 36

Kelso, Frank, 87
Kennedy, John F., 94
Khaled, Fathia Nouri (first wife), 50
Khomeini, Ayatollah, 76
Kikhia, Mansour, 90
Kim Jong II, 64

111

INDEX

Kissinger, Henry, 74
Koran, 25, 26, 44, 46, 50

Laqueur, Walter, 79
Lebanon
 and Egypt, 36
 and Qaddafi supporting terrorist acts in Beirut, 76
Libya
 as colony, 34–35
 and flora and fauna, 30–31
 and geography, 27–30, 52
 and history, 20–23, 52
 and independence, 23, 37
 as monarchy, 23–25. *See also* Idris I
 and religion, 25–27
 See also Qaddafi, Muammar
Libyan Arab Republic, Qaddafi establishing, 42
Libyan Army
 and Libya's militarization, 51, 63, 65–66
 and Qaddafi as colonel, 42
 and Qaddafi as commander, 44
 and Qaddafi as lieutenant, 39
 Qaddafi's classmates in, 39
 and sanctions, 82
 and Soviet Union supporting, 82, 87, 88, 94, 95
 and United States bombing Libya, 87–88, 90
 women in, 51
Libyan Jihad Center for Historical Studies, 105
Little, Douglas, 56–57, 95, 96
local people's committees, 19
Lockerbie, Scotland. *See* Pan Am Flight 103
Luata, 20
Lycett, Andrew, 88, 89, 90

Mandela, Nelson, 69, 84
Mecca
 Muhammad born in, 25
 pilgrimage to, 27
Megrahi, Abdelbaset Ali Mohmed al-, 70–72, 80, 84
militarization of Libya, 51, 63, 65–66
Mohammed, Mohammed Abdul Salam bin Hamed bin ("Abu Meniar") (father), 34–35
Morocco
 and Egypt, 36
 and Qaddafi desiring one unified Arab state, 75
Mosque of Gamal Abdel Nasser, 61
Muhammad, 25–26, 27, 34

Nasser, Gamal Abdel, 36–37, 42, 50, 61, 65
national character, 22–23
National Front for the Salvation of Libya, 104
Nefusa, 20
neighborhoods, and Qaddafi, 18
New Era, Qadaffi on, 12–14, 17–19, 96–97, 99–104
New York Times, The, 72, 82
Newyorker.com, 97, 101
Nidal, Abu, 76–77
North Korea, and Libya's destruction of weapons of mass destruction, 101
Northern Ireland, and Qaddafi supporting Irish Republican Army, 75
nuclear weapons, Qadaffi agreeing to destruction and confiscation of, 17–18, 99, 101–102. *See also* weapons of mass destruction

112

INDEX

Occidental Petroleum, 56–57
oil, 30, 52–57
    and CIA, 94
    current status of, 57
    discovery of, 14, 16, 24, 52–53, 93
    and European Union, 65
    and Idris I, 24, 94–95
    and Qaddafi, 14, 18, 51, 53–57, 79, 81, 86, 95, 97
    and Qaddafi paying Carlos the Jackel to kidnap oil ministers from Saudi Arabia and Iran, 75
    and Qaddafi's demands on foreign companies, 56–57
    and sanctions, 63, 72, 81, 86
    and Soviet Union, 67
    and United States, 44, 65, 68, 103
Olympics (Munich, Germany), and Qaddafi supporting Black September Group's attack on Israeli athletes, 72–74, 75
Order of Good Hope Award, Qaddafi receiving, 69
Organization of Petroleum Exporting Countries (OPEC), 56–57

Palestine
    and Qaddafi preventing peace with Israel, 63–64, 67
    and Qaddafi supporting terrorist group of Abu Nidal, 76–77
Palestine Liberation Organization (PLO), 67
    and Black September Group's attack on Israeli athletes at Olympics, 72–74
    and Qaddafi, 16, 100
Palestinians, returning Israel to, 25

Pan Am Flight 103, bombing of, 16, 70–72, 80–81, 82
    deaths from, 16, 70
    and Libya accepting responsibility for, 17, 97, 102
    and Libya paying restitution to families, 17, 81, 97
    and Libya turning over suspects, 84
    and Libyans indicted, 71, 80
    Libyans linked to, 70–71
    and Qaddafi refusing to extradite suspects, 71–72, 80, 82
    Qaddafi supporting, 63, 72
    and trial of suspects, 84
    and United Nations imposing sanctions, 16, 63, 69, 72, 80–82, 97
    and United Nations lifting sanctions, 84, 97
Paris Conference, 68, 76
Philippines, Qaddafi supporting Islamic wars in, 96
Phoenicians, 20–21
Poindexter, John, 90
political party, 49

Qaddadfa tribe, 33
Qaddafi, Hamis (son), 89
Qaddafi, Hanna (adopted daughter), 15, 89
Qaddafi, Muammar
    and aggression against neighbors, 63, 65–66, 75–76
    and appearance, 12
    assassination attempt against, 69
    birth of, 32
    childhood of, 34–36, 63
    and children, 16, 50, 89, 102
    as colonel in Army, 42

113

INDEX

coup attempts against, 68–69
and coup overthrowing Idris I, 12, 14, 36, 37–39, 41–44, 61, 95
and democracy, 18–19, 104–105
and early political awareness, 36–37
and economy, 14, 16, 18, 44, 46–47, 48–49, 51, 53–57, 63, 69, 102, 103, 105
education of, 34, 35–36, 37–39
and extremism, 14, 16, 51, 61–63
family of, 33–34
and Federation of Arab Republics, 65
and first revolutionary cells, 14, 37
and foreign aggression, 63, 65
and human rights, 102, 103–104
and improvements to Libya, 14, 51, 53–56
and Islam, 12–13, 14, 34, 39, 44–45, 46, 47–48, 49–50, 51, 95, 96
as leader of rogue nation, 63–65
and leadership style, 49–50
and legacy, 104–105
as lieutenant in Army, 39
and marriages, 50
and militarization of Libya, 51, 63, 65–66
and nationalism, 14, 23, 34, 37
and New Era, 12–14, 17–19, 96–97, 98–104
and oil, 14, 18, 51, 53–57, 79, 81, 86, 95, 97
opposition to, 50, 51, 62, 63–66, 68–69, 74, 76, 82, 85
and Order of Good Hope Award from South Africa, 69
and personal guard, 12, 47
and personality, 37, 40, 61–63, 69
and philosophy of government, 14, 36, 42, 44–51, 95–96
and population shift to cities, 50
as prime minister, 44
and religious tolerance, 46
as ruler of Libya, 12, 18–19, 40, 44–51, 104–105
and structure of government, 49
supporters of, 50, 51, 69, 85, 91, 96
and United Arab Nation, 14, 16, 23, 36, 41, 44, 61, 75, 77
and United States bombing Libya, 14, 16, 79, 87–92.
See also terrorism; United Nations; United States
Qaddafi, Saif-al-Arab (son), 89
Qaddafi, Seif al-Islam el- (son), 102
Qaddafi, Sifiiya (second wife), 50
Qaddafi Foundation for Charitable Organizations, 102

Ramadan, 27
Rauf, Imam Feisal Abdul, 27
Reagan, Ronald, 16, 67–68, 77, 79, 87, 89, 90, 91–92
Red Desert (*Hamadah al-Hamra*), 28
religion, 25–27.
See also Islam
revolutionary cells, Qaddafi forming, 37
Revolutionary Command Council (RCC), Qaddafi establishing, 44, 49
Revolutionary Leader, Qaddafi as, 49
Rida, Hassan, 42–43, 44
roads, and Qaddafi, 14, 54, 55, 102
rock paintings, 20

INDEX

rogue nation, Qaddafi as leader of, 63–65
Roman Catholic Cathedral of the Sacred Heart of Jesus, 61
Roman Catholicism, 25
Romans, 21, 31, 52
Rome, and Qaddafi supporting bombings in airports, 14, 74, 76–77

sabkhas, 28
Sadat, Anwar, 65, 66–67, 74, 75–76
Sahara Desert, 32, 52, 53
Salat, 27
sanctions
    United Nations imposing, 16, 17, 63, 69, 72, 80–82, 84, 97
    United Nations lifting, 17, 84, 97
    United States imposing, 14, 16, 17, 56, 63, 68, 69, 82, 84, 84–87, 97
    United States lifting, 17, 103
Sanctions Act against Libya and Iran, 82, 84
Sanusi, Sidi Muhammad Ibn-Ali as-, 26, 34
Saudi Arabia
    and Egypt, 36
    and Mecca, 25, 27
    and Qaddafi paying Carlos the Jackel to kidnap oil ministers, 75
Sawm, 27
Sebha preparatory school, Qaddafi attending, 37–38
sebkhas, 52
Secret Service, 72
Shahada, 27
Shariah, 14, 27, 46
Sharon, Ariel, 67
Shiites, 25
Shultz, George, 91

Sidra, Gulf of, United States conflict with Libya in, 77, 79, 84–85
Sirte, Qaddafi's early years in, 32–36, 37
Socialism
    growth of, 25
    and Qaddafi, 44–45, 46
Socialist People's Libyan Arab Jamahiriya, Libya as, 49
South Africa, Qaddafi receiving Good Hope Award from, 69
Soviet Union
    and Afghanistan invasion, 76
    and Cold War, 93–94
    fall of, 97
    and Libya's independence, 23
    and oil, 67
    Qaddafi against, 46
    and support of Libyan Army, 82, 87, 88, 94, 95
    and support to Libya, 66, 67
    and support to Yemen and Ethiopia, 67
    and United States bombing Libya, 16
Sterling, Claire, 77
Stone Age man, 20
Sudan
    Libya invading, 66–67
    and Qaddafi desiring one unified Arab state, 75
Sunna, 25
Sunni Muslims, 25, 34, 44–45. *See also* Islam
Syria
    and Egypt, 36
    and Libya's destruction of weapons of mass destruction, 101
    and Qaddafi desiring one unified Arab state, 75

INDEX

Tanter, Raymond, 64–65, 67, 81, 84
terrorism, Qaddafi supporting, 12, 62, 63, 67, 70–77, 79, 82, 96, 97
   beginning of, 72–76
   and bombing at West German disco, 14, 63, 79
   and economy, 57
   escalation of, 14, 16, 76–77, 79
   and opposition to Qaddafi, 51, 62, 63–66, 74
   Qaddafi's speech on cessation of, 12–14, 17–19, 100–101
   and Quadaffi as rogue leader, 63–65
   and training camps, 63, 79, 89
   and United Nations imposing sanctions, 16, 63, 69, 72, 80–82, 97
   and United States bombing Libya, 14, 16, 79, 87–92
   and United States imposing sanctions, 14, 16, 17, 56, 63, 69, 84–87, 97.
   See also Pan Am Flight 103; weapons of mass destruction
Thatcher, Margaret, 90
Third Universal Theory, 14, 46, 96
Third Way, 96
Tibesti Mountains, 28
Time magazine, 31
Tobruk, 28
tourism, 31, 103
transportation, and Qaddafi, 55, 56, 102
tribes, 34, 50, 52
tribes (*qabilah*), 22–23
Tripoli, 27–28, 30
   and attack on American Embassy, 76
   and Idris I, 23
   United States bombing, 14, 16, 87, 89

Tripolitania, 23, 28, 34
Tunisia, 22
   and Egypt, 36
   Libya in conflict with, 63, 65–66
   and Qaddafi desiring one unified Arab state, 75
Turks, 22
Tyre, 20

unemployment, and Qaddafi, 18, 102
United Kingdom, and United States bombing Libya, 91
United Kingdom of Libya, 23
United Nations
   and diplomatic relations with Libya, 103–104
   and imposing sanctions, 16, 63, 69, 72, 80–82, 84
   and Libya's independence, 23, 35
   and lifting sanctions, 17, 84, 97, 103
   and United States bombing Libya, 91
United States
   and aid to Libya before oil discovery, 53
   and air base in Libya, 93–95
   and bombing Libya, 14, 16, 79, 87–92
   and CIA aiding opposition groups in Libya, 76
   and discontinuing diplomatic relations with Libya, 96
   and discovery of oil, 53
   and Gulf of Sidra conflict, 77, 79, 84, 86
   and Idris I, 24
   and imposing sanctions, 14, 16, 17, 56, 63, 68, 69, 82, 84, 84–87
   and Israel, 57

INDEX

and Libya as rogue nation, 65
and Libya giving up its weapons of mass destruction and nuclear plans, 17–18, 98, 100, 101–102
and Libya's independence, 23
and lifting sanctions, 17, 18
and military bases in Libya, 24
and oil, 56–57, 65, 68, 94
and Paris Conference, 68
and Qaddaffi supporting hyjacking of American cruise ship and killing of elderly American, 76
Qaddafi against, 13, 14
and Qaddafi bombing disco in West Germany, 14, 63, 79
and Qaddafi bombing Rome airport in lieu of killing Kissinger, 74
Qaddafi reinstituting relations with, 16, 17–18, 96–97, 99–104
and Qaddafi supporting Black Panthers, 75
and Qaddafi supporting killing of American pilot and passengers on plane, 76
and Qaddafi supporting terrorist acts in Beirut, Lebanon, 76
and Reagan, 16, 67–68, 77, 79, 87, 89, 90, 91–92
and reinstituting diplomatic relations, 18, 31
and shooting down two Libyan Air Force jets, 79, 85
and sinking two Libyan patrol boats
and support of Qaddafi's coup, 42, 44
and World War II, 23, 32

U.S. News & World Report, 17, 18
University of Libya, Qaddafi attending, 39
USnews.com, 101, 105

Vandals, 22
vegetation, in Libya, 31
Vienna, bombings in airports in, 14
Voice of the Arabs, 36

wadden, 30
wadis, 52
Wakin, Edward, 79
water supply, 58–60
wealth, Qaddafi on, 46–47
weapons of mass destruction
  and international weapons inspectors, 97, 99
  and Libya as rogue nation, 64–65
  and Libya in talks with Britain giving up development of, 17, 99
  and Paris Conference, 68
  Qaddafi agreeing to destruction and confiscation of, 17–18, 98, 100, 101–102
  Qaddafi supporting production of, 63
  and United States imposing sanctions, 14, 16, 17, 56, 63, 68, 69, 82, 84, 84–87, 97
Weinberger, Caspar, 92
Weldon, Curt, 101
West
  and Nasser, 36–37
  Qaddafi against, 14, 31, 39, 46, 49–50, 67–68, 76–77, 91, 95, 96
  Qaddafi reaching out to, 96–97, 99–104.
  See also United States

117

INDEX

West Berlin disco, bombing in, 14, 63, 79
West Germany
   and Qaddafi supporting Black September Group's attack on athletes at Olympics, 72–74, 75
   Qaddafi supporting bombing disco in, 14, 63, 79
   and United States bombing Libya, 91
Wheelus Field, 93–95
Willis, Terri, 44

women
   in Army, 51
   Qaddafi on, 12, 14, 47–48
workplace, Qaddafi on, 48–49
World Trade Center attacks, Qaddafi denouncing, 96
World War II, 23, 32, 35, 53

Yemen
   and Egypt, 36
   Soviet Union supporting, 67

Zakat, 27

PICTURE CREDITS

page:
- 11: Courtesy University of Texas, Austin
- 13: Associated Press/AP
- 15: Associated Press/AP
- 21: © AFP/Getty Images
- 24: Associated Press/AP
- 29: © Getty Images
- 33: © Time Life Pictures/Getty Images
- 35: © Genevieve Chauvel/Sygma/CORBIS
- 38: © Bettmann/CORBIS
- 43: Associated Press, AP
- 45: © Genevieve Chauvel/Sygma/CORBIS
- 48: © Christine Spengler/CORBIS
- 54: © Getty Images
- 59: © Time Life Pictures/Getty Images
- 62: Associated Press/AP
- 66: © Bettmann/CORBIS
- 71: © Getty Images
- 73: Associated Press/AP
- 78: © Reuters/CORBIS
- 83: © Getty Images
- 85: © Lorenzo Ciniglio/CORBIS
- 88: AFP/Getty Images
- 94: © Time Life Pictures/Getty Images
- 98: © Reuters/CORBIS
- 103: Associated Press/AP

Cover: © Bettmann/CORBIS
Frontis: © Alain Nogues/CORBIS SYGMA

ABOUT THE CONTRIBUTORS

BRENDA LANGE has been a journalist, an author, and a public relations professional for more than 15 years. During that time, she has written for newspapers, magazines, and trade publications, and performed public relations functions for various nonprofit agencies. She received her bachelor's degree from Temple University in Philadelphia, and is a member of the American Society of Journalists and Authors, the National Writers Union, and the International Women's Writing Guild. This book is her third for Chelsea House Publishers. Lange lives in Doylestown, PA, with her husband and their children.

ARTHUR M. SCHLESINGER, jr. is the leading American historian of our time. He won the Pulitzer Prize for his book *The Age of Jackson* (1945) and again for a chronicle of the Kennedy administration, *A Thousand Days* (1965), which also won the National Book Award. Professor Schlesinger is the Albert Schweitzer Professor of the Humanities at the City University of New York and has been involved in several other Chelsea House projects, including the series REVOLUTIONARY WAR LEADERS, COLONIAL LEADERS, and YOUR GOVERNMENT.